Collins

AQA GCSE 9-1
Biology
Foundation

Practice Papers

Mike Smith and Kath Skillern

Contents

SET A

Paper 1 3

Paper 2 27

SET B

Paper 1 51

Paper 2 75

ANSWERS 99

Acknowledgements

The authors and publisher are grateful to the copyright holders for permission to use quoted materials and images.

All images are © HarperCollins*Publishers* and Shutterstock.com

Every effort has been made to trace copyright holders and obtain their permission for the use of copyright material. The author and publisher will gladly receive information enabling them to rectify any error or omission in subsequent editions. All facts are correct at time of going to press.

Published by Collins
An imprint of HarperCollins*Publishers*
1 London Bridge Street
London SE1 9GF

© HarperCollins*Publishers* Limited 2019

ISBN 9780008321406

First published 2019

This edition published 2020

British Library Cataloguing in Publication Data.

A CIP record of this book is available from the British Library.

Commissioning Editor: Kerry Ferguson
Project Leader and Management: Chantal Addy and Shelley Teasdale
Authors: Mike Smith and Kath Skillern
Cover Design: Sarah Duxbury
Inside Concept Design: Ian Wrigley
Text Design and Layout: QBS Learning
Production: Karen Nulty
Printed by CPI Group (UK) Ltd, Croydon CR0 4YY

MIX
Paper from responsible source
FSC™ C007454

This book is produced from independently certified FSC™ paper to ensure responsible forest management.

For more information visit:
www.harpercollins.co.uk/green

Collins

AQA
GCSE
Biology
SET A – Paper 1 Foundation Tier

Author: Mike Smith

F

Materials

Time allowed: 1 hour 45 minutes

> **For this paper you must have:**
> - a ruler
> - a calculator.

Instructions

- Answer **all** questions in the spaces provided.
- Do all rough work in this book. Cross through any work you do not want to be marked.

Information

- There are 100 marks available on this paper.
- The marks for questions are shown in brackets.
- You are expected to use a calculator where appropriate.
- You are reminded of the need for good English and clear presentation in your answers.
- When answering questions 05.3, 10.3 and 12.3 you need to make sure that your answer:
  - is clear, logical, sensibly structured
  - fully meets the requirements of the question
  - shows that each separate point or step supports the overall answer

Advice

- In all calculations, show clearly how you work out your answer.

Name: ....

01 **Figure 1.1** shows four types of cell.

Figure 1.1

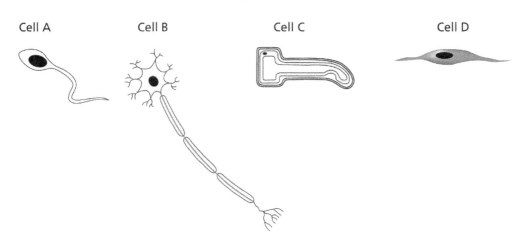

Cell A   Cell B   Cell C   Cell D

01.1 Which cell is a nerve cell?

Give **one** reason for your answer.

Cell _____

Reason _____ **[2 marks]**

01.2 Which cell is a root hair cell?

Give **one** reason for your answer.

Cell _____

Reason _____ **[2 marks]**

01.3 Which cell is a sperm cell?

Give **one** reason for your answer.

Cell _____

Reason _____ **[2 marks]**

01.4 Which cell comes from a plant?

Give **one** reason for your answer.

Cell _____

Reason _____ **[2 marks]**

02   Plants make glucose when they photosynthesise.

02.1 Which of the following is **not** used for photosynthesis?

Tick **one** box.

Carbon dioxide ☐

Light ☐

Oxygen ☐

Water ☐

[1 mark]

02.2 Where does most photosynthesis take place in a plant?

Tick **one** box.

Epidermal tissue ☐

Palisade mesophyll ☐

Phloem ☐

Xylem ☐

[1 mark]

02.3 What is the chemical symbol for glucose?

Tick **one** box.

$C_6H_6O_{12}$ ☐

$C_6H_{12}O_6$ ☐

$C_{12}H_6O_6$ ☐

$C_{12}H_6O_{12}$ ☐

[1 mark]

Question 2 continues on the next page

02.4 Plants can convert glucose to other substances.

Draw **one** line from each substance to its use.

Substance made from glucose   **Use**

Amino acids		Food storage
Cellulose		Protein synthesis
Starch		Strengthen cell walls

[2 marks]

02.5 Some of the glucose made in photosynthesis is converted to other sugars.

Use words from the box to complete the sentences.

| active transport | osmosis | phloem |
| spongy mesophyll | translocation | xylem |

Sugars are transported from the leaves to other parts of the plant through the

_____ .

This movement of sugars is called _____ . **[2 marks]**

02.6 At which time of day do plants photosynthesise most?

Tick **one** box.

Midnight ☐

Early morning ☐

Midday ☐

Early evening ☐

Give **two** reasons for your answer.

1. _____

2. _____ **[3 marks]**

03 The blood system is made of different parts.

03.1 Draw **one** line from each part of the blood to its function.

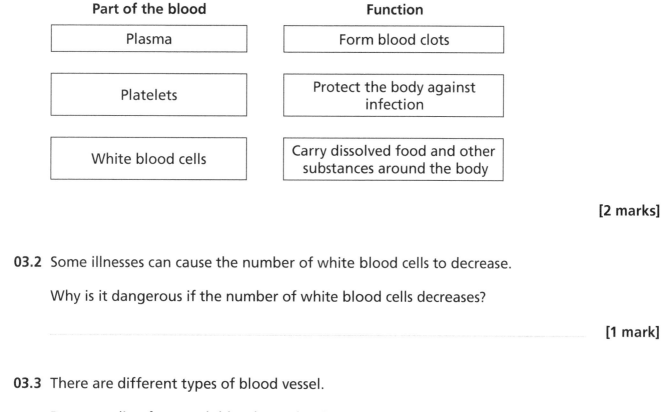

Part of the blood

Plasma

Platelets

White blood cells

Function

Form blood clots

Protect the body against infection

Carry dissolved food and other substances around the body

[2 marks]

03.2 Some illnesses can cause the number of white blood cells to decrease.

Why is it dangerous if the number of white blood cells decreases?

_____

[1 mark]

03.3 There are different types of blood vessel.

Draw **one** line from each blood vessel to its structure.

The diagrams are **not** to scale.

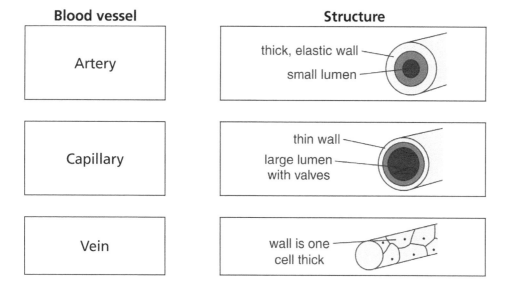

Blood vessel

Artery

Capillary

Vein

Structure

thick, elastic wall
small lumen

thin wall
large lumen
with valves

wall is one
cell thick

[2 marks]

Question 3 continues on the next page

03.4 In coronary heart disease there is **reduced** blood flow to the heart muscle.

Explain why it is dangerous if there is **reduced** blood flow to the heart muscle.

....

....

.... **[2 marks]**

03.5 Treatments for coronary heart disease include the following:

Artificial heart	Drug treatment	Replacement heart valve	Stent

A patient has suffered heart failure, but no suitable donor is available.

Which of these treatments should the patient have?

Explain your answer.

Treatment ....

Reason ....

.... **[2 marks]**

04 Malaria is a disease caused by a single-celled pathogen called *Plasmodium*.

Mosquitoes take in *Plasmodium* when they feed on an infected person.

They can then pass on *Plasmodium* to the next person they feed on.

04.1 Figure 4.1 shows the life cycle of mosquitoes.

Mosquitoes lay their eggs in still water.

Figure 4.1

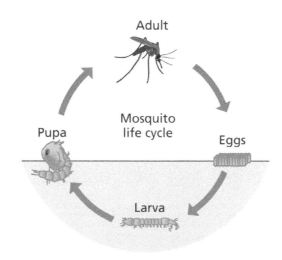

Suggest how **both** of the following help control the spread of malaria.

Spraying still water with oil to cover the surface.

_____

_____

Wearing long sleeves and long trousers.

_____

_____ **[2 marks]**

Question 4 continues on the next page

04.2 A type of mosquito that can spread malaria lives in the UK.

However, malaria is rare in the UK.

Suggest why these mosquitoes do **not** usually spread malaria in the UK.

_____

_____

_____ **[2 marks]**

04.3 Other diseases are caused by different types of pathogen.

Draw **one** line from each disease to the type of pathogen that causes it.

Disease	Type of pathogen
Measles	Bacterial
Rose black spot	Fungal
Salmonella food poisoning	Viral

[2 marks]

04.4 **Figure 4.2** shows a *Plasmodium* cell.

Figure 4.2

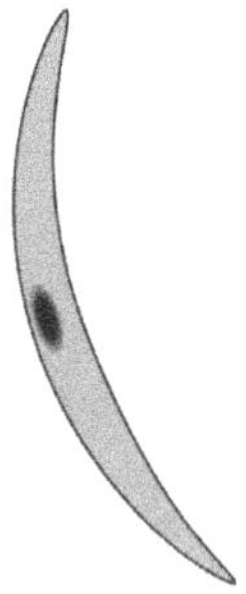

Plasmodium is a protist.

It is bigger than a bacterial cell.

Give **two other** ways it is different from a bacterial cell.

1. _____

2. _____ **[2 marks]**

05   Many medical drugs were originally extracted from plants and microorganisms.

05.1 Draw **one** line from each drug to the organism that originally produced it.

Drug	Organism
Aspirin	Foxglove plant
Digitalis	*Penicillium* mould
Penicillin	Willow tree

[2 marks]

05.2 Today most new drugs are made by chemists.

Suggest **two** reasons why most new drugs today are made by chemists and **not** extracted from organisms like plants.

1. ....

....

2. ....

.... [2 marks]

Question 5 continues on the next page

05.3 Doctors investigated whether taking aspirin affects the risk of getting cancer.

Volunteers taking part in the study took a daily dose of aspirin or a placebo.

Figure 5.1 shows the results.

Figure 5.1

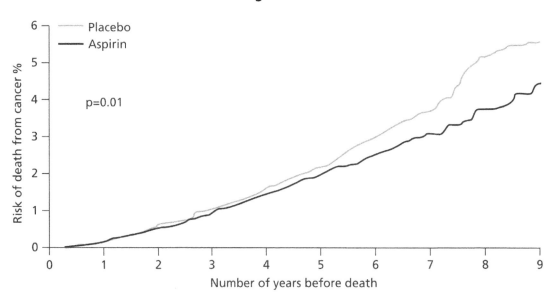

Use **Figure 5.1** to **describe** the effect of taking aspirin on the risk of dying from cancer.

....

....

....

....

....

....

....

[4 marks]

06   Yeast is used in the production of alcoholic drinks.

Yeast converts glucose to ethanol (alcohol) during anaerobic respiration.

06.1 What is another word for anaerobic respiration in yeast?

Tick **one** box.

Differentiation ☐

Diffusion ☐

Fermentation ☐

Ventilation ☐

[1 mark]

06.2 Figure 6.1 shows a container used to make beer.

Figure 6.1

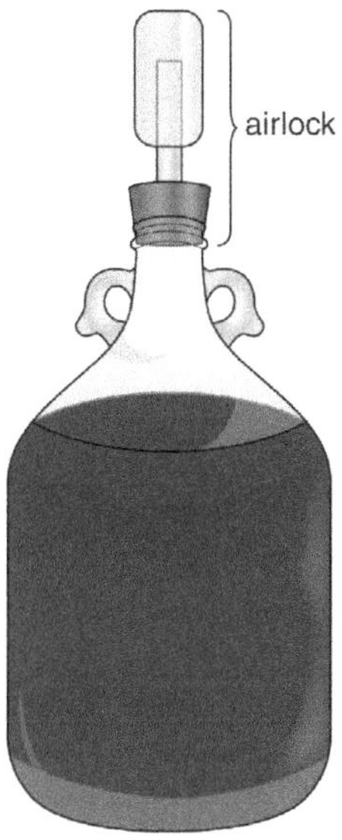

The airlock prevents any gases entering the container.

Suggest why this is necessary.

_____

_____

_____ [2 marks]

Question 6 continues on the next page

06.3 The airlock does allow gases to leave the container.

Suggest why this is necessary.

_____

_____

_____ **[2 marks]**

06.4 Write the word equation for anaerobic respiration in **human muscles**.

_____ **[2 marks]**

06.5 Humans do **not** just use anaerobic respiration.

They mainly use aerobic respiration.

Give **one** reason why humans do **not** just use anaerobic respiration.

_____

_____ **[1 mark]**

07   Bacteria multiply by cell division.

07.1 Bacteria can divide every 20 minutes.

If you start with one bacterial cell, how many cells will there be after 1 hour?

Tick **one** box.

2   ☐

4   ☐

6   ☐

8   ☐

[1 mark]

07.2 A student grew bacterial colonies on an agar plate using the following method.

1. Pass an inoculating loop through a Bunsen flame.

2. Let the loop cool.

3. Dip the loop in a bacterial culture.

4. Slightly lift the lid off an agar plate.

5. Use the loop to spread some of the bacterial culture over the agar.

6. Pass the loop through the Bunsen flame again.

7. Seal the lid of the agar plate with adhesive tape, but **not** all the way round.

8. Store the agar plate upside down.

9. Incubate the agar plate at 25°C

Explain the reasons for steps 1, 2, 8 and 9

Reason for step 1

Reason for step 2

Reason for step 8

Reason for step 9

[4 marks]

Question 7 continues on the next page

07.3 Another student spread a bacterial culture evenly over an agar plate.

Four filter paper discs, A–D, were impregnated with different antibiotics.

The four paper discs were placed on the agar plate before it was incubated.

Figure 7.1 shows the results. The shaded area shows where bacteria are present.

Figure 7.1

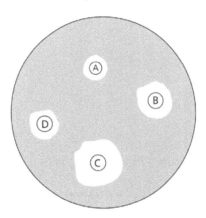

Which antibiotic is the most effective at preventing the growth of the bacteria?

Give a reason for your answer.

Antibiotic ....

Reason ....

.... **[2 marks]**

07.4 The student needed to measure the diameter of each clear zone to work out its area.

For each clear zone, the student took several measurements of the diameter.

Explain why this was necessary.

....

....

.... **[2 marks]**

08   **Figure 8.1** shows a cactus plant.

Figure 8.1

08.1 Some cactus plants have spines and a thick waxy coating on the stem.

These adaptations help to conserve water.

Explain **one other** way that **each** of these adaptations help cactus plants survive.

Spines ....

....

Waxy coating ....

.... **[4 marks]**

08.2 As well as water, cactus plants also need mineral ions, like magnesium.

How will a cactus be affected if it does **not** have enough magnesium?

Explain your answer.

....

....

.... **[2 marks]**

Turn over >

09   Scientists made a new trachea for a patient whose own had been damaged by cancer.

They grew the new trachea using stem cells from the patient's own bone marrow.

09.1 Use words from the box to complete the sentences.

abnormal	benign	genetic
malignant	tissues	

Cancer tumours are formed by uncontrolled cell growth.

Tumours that spread to other parts of the body are called ....

Tumours that stay in one area are called ....   **[2 marks]**

09.2 What is the function of the trachea?

....

....   **[1 mark]**

09.3 What are stem cells?

....

....

....   **[2 marks]**

09.4 The scientists used stem cells from bone marrow.

Some people have objections to using some other types of stem cell.

Explain why they have objections.

....

....

....   **[1 mark]**

09.5 Suggest **one** benefit of using the patient's **own** stem cells.

....   **[1 mark]**

10   Many diseases can be treated with medicines.

10.1   The common cold is caused by a virus.

Doctors give medicines like aspirin to patients with a cold.

Doctors do **not** give antibiotics to patients with a cold.

Explain why patients with a cold should take a medicine like aspirin.

....

....

Explain why patients with a cold should **not** take antibiotics.

....

....   **[2 marks]**

10.2   New medicines have to be tested in clinical trials before they can be used for the general public.

Give **two** reasons why new drugs have to be tested.

1. ....

....

2. ....

....   **[2 marks]**

Question 10 continues on the next page

10.3 Some clinical trials of new medicines use healthy volunteers, and some use ill patients.

Many clinical trials involve the use of placebos.

Should you use placebos with both healthy volunteers and ill patients?

Explain your answer.

[4 marks]

10.4 Some clinical trials are double blind trials.

Why are double blind trials used?

[1 mark]

11 Microscopes can be used to study very small structures.

11.1 **Figure 11.1** shows some structures of different sizes.

The diagrams are **not** to scale.

Figure 11.1

| 2 cm | 7 μm | 100 nm | 3 mm |
| acorn | red blood cell | virus | ant |

Write the objects in order of their size, from the smallest to the largest.

Smallest ....

....

....

Largest .... **[2 marks]**

Question 11 continues on the next page

11.2 **Figure 11.2** shows an image of a white blood cell.

Figure 11.2

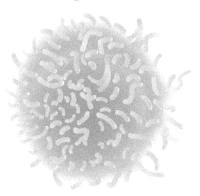

The actual size of the cell is 12 µm

The diameter of the image is 60 mm

Calculate the magnification of the image.

Use the formula:

$$\text{magnification} = \frac{\text{size of image}}{\text{size of real object}}$$

Magnification: .... **[3 marks]**

11.3 When using a microscope to view cells:

- often a stain is used

- the cells are first viewed using low power.

Explain the reason for each of these.

Reason for using a stain: ....

Reason for viewing first with low power: ....

[2 marks]

12   **Figure 12.1** shows the apparatus that a student used to investigate transpiration.

Figure 12.1

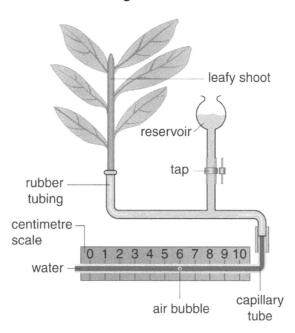

Table 12.1 shows the student's results.

Table 12.1

Time in min	Distance air bubble moved in mm
0	0
5	18
10	25
15	54
20	72

Question 12 continues on the next page

12.1 Plot the data from **Table 12.1** onto **Figure 12.2**

Circle any anomalous results.

Draw a line of best fit.

Figure 12.2

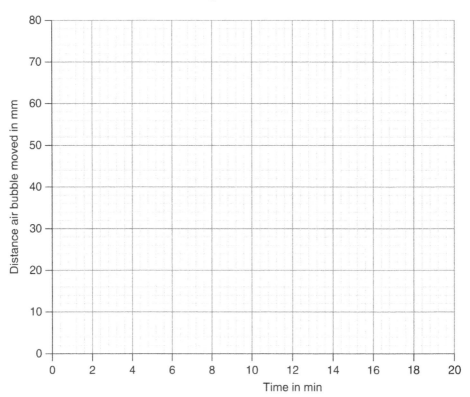

[4 marks]

12.2 Explain why transpiration caused the air bubble to move.

_____

[1 mark]

12.3 The rate of transpiration is affected by air movement.

Describe a method you could use to investigate this.

Include the apparatus shown in **Figure 12.1**, plus an electric fan to produce air movement.

You should include:

- what you would measure

- variables you would control.

[6 marks]

END OF QUESTIONS

BLANK PAGE

AQA

GCSE

Biology

F

SET A – Paper 2 Foundation Tier

Author: Mike Smith

Materials

Time allowed: 1 hour 45 minutes

> **For this paper you must have:**
> - a ruler
> - a calculator.

Instructions

- Answer **all** questions in the spaces provided.
- Do all rough work in this book. Cross through any work you do not want to be marked.

Information

- There are 100 marks available on this paper.
- The marks for questions are shown in brackets.
- You are expected to use a calculator where appropriate.
- You are reminded of the need for good English and clear presentation in your answers.
- When answering questions 09.3, 11.4 and 12.1 you need to make sure that your answer:
  - is clear, logical, sensibly structured
  - fully meets the requirements of the question
  - shows that each separate point or step supports the overall answer.

Advice

- In all calculations, show clearly how you work out your answer.

Name: ....

---

01 The body monitors and controls its temperature and water content.

01.1 Which responses occur when body temperature is too high?

Tick **two** boxes.

Blood vessels constrict (get narrower) ☐

Blood vessels dilate (get wider) ☐

Heart rate increases ☐

Muscles shiver ☐

Sweat is produced ☐

[2 marks]

01.2 Use words from the box to complete the sentences.

blood	brain	eyes	surroundings	urine

Responses that happen when the body temperature is too high are controlled by the

thermoregulatory centre in the _____ .

This detects that the temperature is too high by monitoring the temperature of the

_____ .

[2 marks]

01.3 Some processes increase the amount of water in the body.

Other processes decrease the amount of water.

Put ticks (✓) in **Table 1.1** to show whether each process increases or decreases the amount of water in the body.

Table 1.1

Process	Increases water in the body	Decreases water in the body
Breathing		
Eating		
Sweating		
Urinating		

[2 marks]

01.4 Controlling body temperature and the amount of water in the body are examples of what process?

Tick **one** box.

Accommodation ☐

Adaptation ☐

Homeostasis ☐

Osmosis ☐

[1 mark]

Turn over >

02   **Figure 2.1** shows some of the human hormone glands.

Figure 2.1

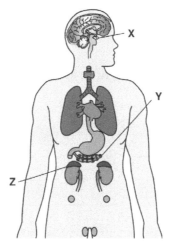

02.1 Write down the names of glands **X**, **Y** and **Z**.

Choose your answers from the list.

Adrenal   Pancreas   Pituitary   Testes   Thyroid

Gland **X**: ....

Gland **Y**: ....

Gland **Z**: ....   **[3 marks]**

02.2 How do hormones travel around the body?

.... **[1 mark]**

02.3 Draw **one** line from each hormone to the gland that secretes it.

Hormone	**Gland**
Insulin	Ovary
Oestrogen	Testis
Testosterone	Pancreas

[2 marks]

02.4 What health condition is caused by a lack of insulin?

.... **[1 mark]**

03 **Figure 3.1** shows part of an Arctic food web.

Figure 3.1

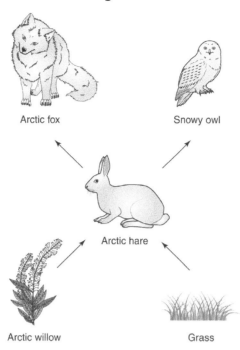

03.1 Write down **one** producer from **Figure 3.1**

.... **[1 mark]**

03.2 Write down **one** secondary consumer from **Figure 3.1**

.... **[1 mark]**

03.3 If the number of Arctic foxes decreased, what would start to happen to the number of snowy owls?

Give a reason for your answer.

Answer: ....

Reason: ....

.... **[2 marks]**

03.4 What term describes all the organisms in the Arctic food web?

Tick **one** box.

Community ☐

Ecosystem ☐

Environment ☐

Habitat ☐

[1 mark]

Question 3 continues on the next page

03.5 Some organisms in the Arctic food web may compete for **biotic** factors.

Which factor can be described as biotic?

Tick **one** box.

Light ☐

Mates ☐

Mineral ions ☐

Water ☐

[1 mark]

03.6 **Figure 3.2** shows an Arctic fox.

Figure 3.2

Arctic foxes are predators.

Identify **one** adaptation that helps an Arctic fox survive as a predator.

Explain how the adaptation helps it survive.

Adaptation: _____

How it helps survival as a predator: _____

_____ **[2 marks]**

03.7 **Figure 3.3** shows an Arctic hare.

Figure 3.3

Arctic hares are prey animals.

Identify **one** adaptation that helps an Arctic hare survive as a prey animal.

Explain how the adaptation helps it survive.

Adaptation: _____

How it helps survival as a prey animal: _____

_____ **[2 marks]**

04   Hormones are involved in human reproduction.

04.1   Draw **one** line from each hormone to its function.

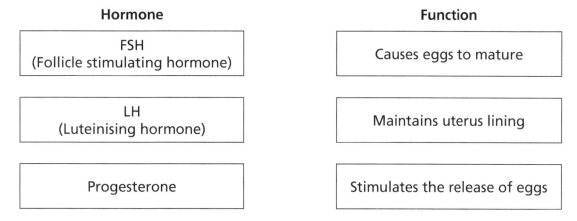

Hormone	Function
FSH (Follicle stimulating hormone)	Causes eggs to mature
LH (Luteinising hormone)	Maintains uterus lining
Progesterone	Stimulates the release of eggs

[2 marks]

04.2   Complete **Table 4.1** to show the number of chromosomes in the different types of human cell.

Table 4.1

Type of cell	Number of chromosomes in cell
Sperm	
Egg	
Fertilised egg	46
Embryo	

[2 marks]

Question 4 continues on the next page

04.3 As an embryo grows, different types of cells develop.

What is this process called?

Tick **one** box.

Differentiation ☐

Fusion ☐

Meiosis ☐

Reproduction ☐

[1 mark]

04.4 Draw **one** line from each contraceptive to how it works.

Contraceptive	How it works
Diaphragm	Kills sperm
Intrauterine device (IUD)	Prevents eggs maturing
Oral contraceptive	Prevents fertilised egg implanting
Spermicide	Prevents sperm reaching egg

[3 marks]

05 Figure 5.1 shows carbon dioxide emissions in California.

Pie chart **B** shows the breakdown of the emissions from transportation.

Figure 5.1

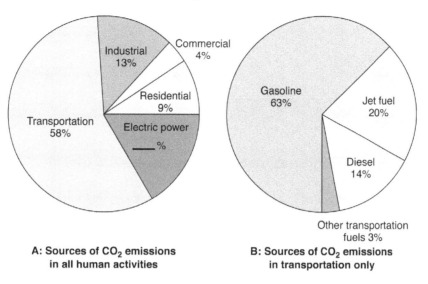

A: Sources of CO_2 emissions
in all human activities

B: Sources of CO_2 emissions
in transportation only

05.1 Calculate the percentage of carbon dioxide emissions from electric power.

Answer = _____ % **[2 marks]**

05.2 Why does using electric power cause carbon dioxide emissions? **[2 marks]**

Question 5 continues on the next page

05.3 Which produces more carbon dioxide emissions, industrial activities **or** jet fuel?

Show your working out to justify your answer. **[2 marks]**

_____

_____

_____

_____

05.4 Why are many people concerned about carbon dioxide emissions? **[1 mark]**

_____

_____

05.5 Which process **removes** carbon dioxide from the atmosphere? **[1 mark]**

Tick **one** box.

Combustion ☐

Deforestation ☐

Photosynthesis ☐

Respiration ☐

06 Variation is caused by the environment or genes.

Figure 6.1 shows some human features that show variation.

Figure 6.1

06.1 Identify **one** feature from **Figure 6.1** that is caused by the environment. **[1 mark]**

_____

06.2 Use words from the box to complete the sentences. **[3 marks]**

chromosome		DNA		double helix
genome	polymer		protein	strand

Genes are made of a chemical called _____ , which forms a shape
called a _____ .

Genes are small sections of a structure called a _____ .

Question 6 continues on the next page

06.3 Earwax can be either wet or dry.

Two alleles control this:

- wet (**A**)

- dry (**a**)

The wet allele is dominant to the dry allele.

Figure 6.2 shows a genetic cross between two people, each with the genotype **Aa**.

Complete **Figure 6.2** [2 marks]

Figure 6.2

	A	a
A		Aa
a		

06.4 What is the **phenotype** of someone with the genotype **Aa**? [1 mark]

06.5 Which term describes someone with the genotype **Aa**? [1 mark]

Tick **one** box.

Dominant ☐

Heterozygous ☐

Homozygous ☐

Recessive ☐

07   Biological factors affect food production.

07.1   Hens that are reared intensively each produce more eggs than free range hens that have more space to move around.

Explain why intensively reared hens produce more eggs than free range hens.

_____

_____

_____ **[2 marks]**

07.2   Eggs from free range hens usually cost more to buy than eggs from intensively farmed hens.

Suggest why they cost more, and why many people are willing to pay this higher price.

Why free range eggs cost more: _____

_____

Why people will pay more: _____

_____ **[2 marks]**

Question 7 continues on the next page

07.3 Food security means having enough food to feed a population.

Draw **one** connecting line from each biological factor to the reason it affects food security.

Biological factor	**Reason it affects food security**
Climate change	Eat or damage crops
Increasing birth rate	Less water available for crops
Pests	More people need food

[2 marks]

07.4 Fish stocks can be conserved in several ways, including:

- fishing quotas

- control of net size

Explain how these measures help conserve fish stocks.

Fishing quotas: ....

....

Control of net size: ....

.... [2 marks]

08   **Figure 8.1** shows a modern breed of cow and a wild cow.

Modern breeds of cow were produced by selective breeding starting with wild cows similar to that shown in **Figure 8.1**

Figure 8.1

Wild cow   Modern breed of cow

08.1 The modern breed of cow has more meat than the wild cow.

Describe how selective breeding can produce a cow with more meat.

_____

_____

_____

_____

_____

_____

_____

_____

                                                        [5 marks]

Question 8 continues on the next page

08.2 Identify **one other** feature in **Figure 8.1** that has been selectively bred for.

Explain why the feature has been selectively bred for.

Feature: ....

Reason: ....

....

[2 marks]

08.3 Some plant crops have been selectively bred.

Other plant crops have been changed by introducing genes from other species.

What is this process called?

Tick **one** box.

Genetic cross ☐

Genetic engineering ☐

Genetic mutation ☐

Genetic variation ☐

[1 mark]

---

09   There are different methods of cloning animals and plants.

Here is the method of cloning animals by embryo transplant:

- selecting a suitable male and female, and breeding them

- collecting the embryo from the **biological mother**, after an egg has been fertilised

- splitting the embryo into separate cells

- growing the cells into separate embryos

- transplanting each embryo into a different **host mother**

- host mothers giving birth to offspring.

09.1 Explain why host mothers are used.

....

.... **[1 mark]**

09.2 The offspring are clones of which animal?

Tick **one** box.

Biological mother ☐

Host mother ☐

Father ☐

Other offspring ☐

[1 mark]

09.3 A garden centre produces new plants by taking cuttings instead of growing them from seeds.

Describe **one advantage** and **one disadvantage** of growing new plants from cuttings compared with growing them from seeds.

....

....

....

....

....

.... **[4 marks]**

Turn over >

10 A student was investigating the effect of gravity on plant growth.

She grew some cress seeds on wet cotton wool in a Petri dish.

When the cress seedlings started to grow, the student turned the dish on its side.

Figure 10.1 shows the results.

Figure 10.1

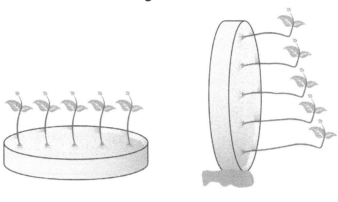

At start

One day after being
turned on its side

10.1 State **one** variable the student should control.

Describe how it should be controlled.

Explain why it is important to control it.

Variable: ....

How the variable should be controlled: ....

....

....

Why it is important to control the variable: ....

....

.... **[3 marks]**

10.2 Explain why it was important to grow more than one seedling.

....

.... **[1 mark]**

10.3 The seedlings grew upwards because of the effect of gravity.

This is controlled by a hormone called auxin.

Auxin moves downwards under the effect of gravity.

Explain how auxin caused the seedlings to grow upwards after the dish was turned on its side.

_____

_____

_____ **[2 marks]**

10.4 The student repeated the experiment.

All the conditions were kept the same as the first time, **except** this time the dish was placed on a device which rotated the dish.

This is shown in **Figure 10.2**

Figure 10.2

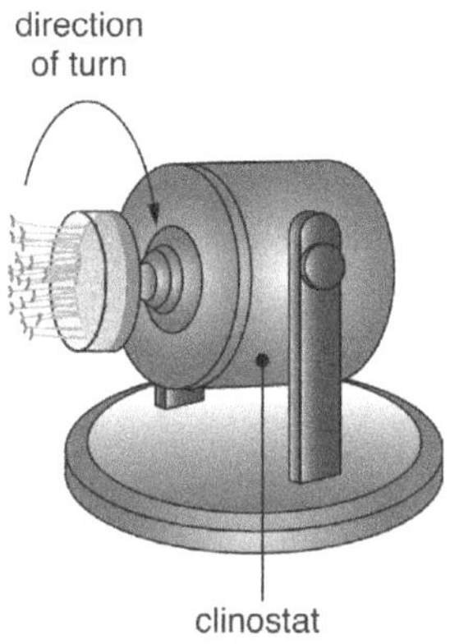

direction
of turn

clinostat

Describe how you would expect the cress seedlings to grow this time.

Explain why the cress seedlings would grow this way.

_____

_____

_____

_____

_____ **[3 marks]**

Turn over >

11   In a park, some grassland is left to grow wild except for a path which is mown regularly.

Students used a transect line to investigate how the path affected the distribution of four different plant species.

Figure 11.1 shows the line of the transect.

The students placed quadrats every metre along the transect.

Figure 11.1

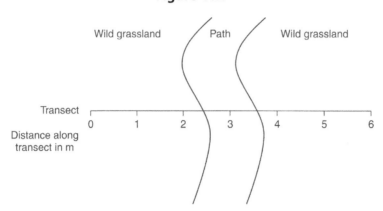

Table 11.1 shows their results.

Table 11.1

Distance along transect in m		0	1	2	3	4	5	6
Number of individual plants of each species per quadrat	Species A	10	8	6	0	8	12	10
	Species B	0	0	2	16	4	0	0
	Species C	8	6	4	0	6	8	8
	Species D	0	0	4	6	2	0	0

11.1   Look at **Table 11.1**

What is the mode number per quadrat for species D?

Answer: _____   **[1 mark]**

11.2   Look at **Table 11.1**

What is the median number per quadrat for species A?

Answer: _____   **[1 mark]**

11.3 **Figure 11.2** shows kite diagrams of the results.

Use the data for **species A** from **Table 11.1** to complete **Figure 11.2**

Figure 11.2

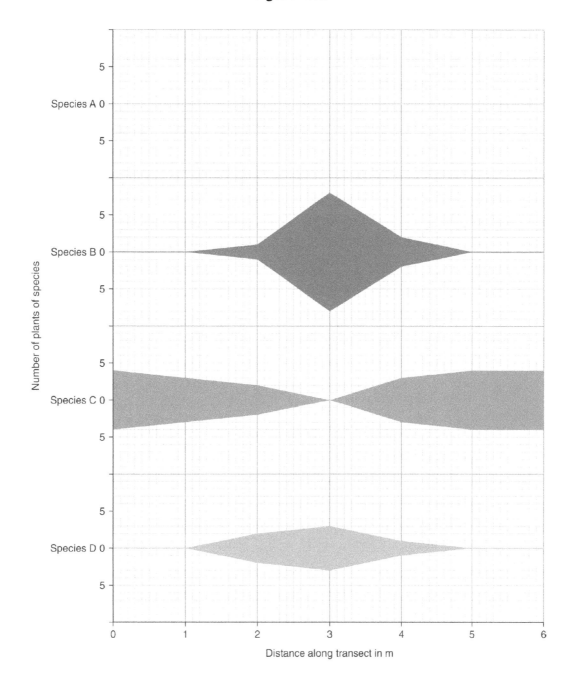

[4 marks]

Question 11 continues on the next page

11.4 **Figure 11.3** shows pictures of each plant species.

Figure 11.3

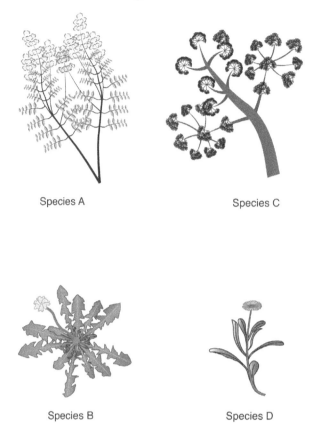

Species A

Species C

Species B

Species D

Suggest reasons for the distributions of the four species along the transect.

Use information from **Table 11.1** and **Figures 11.1**, **11.2** and **11.3** to help you answer.

....

....

....

....

....

....

....

....

[4 marks]

12   A group of students investigated their reaction times.

They each took it in turn to press a timer button as soon as they heard a buzzer.

Each student used their right hand.

Each student took the test three times and recorded their shortest reaction time.

There were eight girls and six boys in the group.

Table 12.1 shows their results.

Table 12.1

	Shortest reaction times in s								Mean reaction time in s
Girls	0.21	0.16	0.18	0.19	0.18	0.16	0.20	0.19	0.18
Boys	0.19	0.15	0.32	0.16	0.17	0.20			0.20

12.1 One of the students made this conclusion:

Girls have shorter reaction times than boys.

Evaluate the method used and the student's conclusion.

_____

_____

_____

_____

_____

_____

_____

_____

_____

_____

_____

                                                                    [6 marks]

Question 12 continues on the next page

12.2 **Figure 12.1** shows the nerve pathway involved in the investigation.

Figure 12.1

Sound of buzzer ⟶ Ear ⟶ Brain ⟶ Hand muscles ⟶ Press button

In **Figure 12.1**, which is the receptor and which is the effector?

Receptor: _____

Effector: _____   **[2 marks]**

12.3 How does information pass along a nerve pathway?

_____

_____ **[2 marks]**

12.4 One of the students says:

Pressing the button quickly is an example of a reflex action.

Is the student correct?

Give a reason for your answer.

Is the student correct? _____

Reason: _____

_____ **[1 mark]**

END OF QUESTIONS

Collins

AQA

GCSE

Biology

F

SET B – Paper 1 Foundation Tier

Author: Kath Skillern

Materials

Time allowed: 1 hour 45 minutes

For this paper you must have:

- a ruler
- a calculator.

Instructions

- Answer **all** questions in the spaces provided.
- Do all rough work in this book. Cross through any work you do not want to be marked.

Information

- There are 100 marks available on this paper.
- The marks for questions are shown in brackets.
- You are expected to use a calculator where appropriate.
- You are reminded of the need for good English and clear presentation in your answers.
- When answering questions 07.5 and 09.2 you need to make sure that your answer:
  - is clear, logical, sensibly structured
  - fully meets the requirements of the question
  - shows that each separate point or step supports the overall answer.

Advice

- In all calculations, show clearly how you work out your answer.

Name: ....

01   Plants can be eaten or damaged by herbivores.

They have chemical and physical methods of defending themselves.

01.1   Which of the following is a **chemical** method used by some plants to defend themselves against being eaten?

Tick **one** box.

Bark ☐

Cellulose cell walls ☐

Poison ☐

Waxy cuticle ☐

[1 mark]

01.2   Some plants defend themselves by mechanical actions.

Draw **one** line from each method of mechanical plant defence to its action.

Mechanical plant defence	**Action**
Mimicry	Curl when touched
Specialised leaves	Difficult to eat
Thorns	Tricks animals

[2 marks]

01.3   What is the first physical barrier a pathogen encounters when attacking a human?

_____

[1 mark]

    ©HarperCollins*Publishers* 2019

01.4 White blood cells help to defend the human body against pathogens.

How do white blood cells help to defend the body?

Tick **one** box.

Alcohol production ☐

Antibiotic production ☐

Antibody production ☐

Antigen production ☐

[1 mark]

01.5 Which of the diagrams below represents a white blood cell?

The diagrams are **not** to scale.

Tick **one** box.

☐ ☐ ☐

[1 mark]

01.6 Describe how antibiotics can be used to treat diseases.

....

....

....

[2 marks]

01.7 Describe how antibiotics are different from painkillers.

....

....

....

[2 marks]

Turn over >

02 Jon has a greenhouse and grows a variety of plants.

He notices that some of his plants appear unhealthy.

02.1 What type of organism causes tobacco mosaic disease in plants?

.... **[1 mark]**

02.2 Describe the appearance of the leaves of a plant suffering from this disease.

....

.... **[1 mark]**

02.3 The attack on the leaves by this disease interferes with photosynthesis.

Describe how this affects the whole plant.

....

.... **[1 mark]**

02.4 Which of these diseases is caused by a fungus?

Tick **one** box.

Aphids ☐

Black spot ☐

Gonorrhoea ☐

Salmonella ☐ **[1 mark]**

02.5 Plants can also be damaged by a lack of certain ions.

A lack of magnesium ions causes chlorosis.

Describe the appearance of a plant with chlorosis.

Explain why it looks this way.

_____

_____ **[2 marks]**

02.6 A lack of nitrate ions causes stunted growth in plants.

Explain why this is.

_____

_____ **[1 mark]**

Turn over >

03   The digestive system is a collection of organs that work together to digest and absorb our food.

03.1   What is the name given to biological molecules that break down our food?

Tick **one** box.

Catalysts ☐

Enzymes ☐

Proteins ☐

Substrate ☐

[1 mark]

03.2 Jon ate a sausage sandwich.

Complete the following sentences:

• Proteases break down proteins to _____ .

• Glycerol and fatty acids are produced when lipases break down

_____ .

[2 marks]

03.3 Amylase is a carbohydrase which breaks down starch to maltose and glucose.

Jon wanted to investigate the effect of pH on the rate of reaction of amylase.

This is the method used.

1. Gather three solutions:

  • amylase

  • starch solution

  • pH buffer solution.

2. Set up a spotting tile with rows of iodine drops and prepare the stopwatch.

3. Mix the three solutions in a test tube in a particular order and start the stopwatch.

Which is the correct order to put the solutions into the test tube?

Tick **one** box.

Buffer first, followed by starch and amylase last ☐

Starch first, followed by amylase and buffer last ☐

Amylase first, followed by buffer solution and starch last ☐

[1 mark]

   ©HarperCollins*Publishers* 2019

03.4 Explain why it is important to mix the solutions in the correct order.

_____

[1 mark]

03.5 Every 10 seconds, Jon used a pipette to place a drop of the mix onto the next iodine drop in the spotting tile.

He repeated this until the iodine remained orange after the mix was added.

He also set up a colour control with iodine and water.

Explain why a control might help.

_____

_____

[2 marks]

03.6 **Table 3.1** shows some results from the investigation.

Table 3.1

pH of solution	5	6	7	8	9
Times for colour change to occur (seconds)					
Test 1	160	75	50	85	85
Test 2	150	70	40	80	95
Test 3	150	75	40	75	90
Mean	153	73	43		90

Calculate the mean time for colour change to occur for the pH 8 solution.

Mean = _____

Units = _____ **[3 marks]**

Question 3 continues on the next page

03.7 Which is the optimum pH for amylase to work?

Tick **one** box.

pH 5 ☐

pH 6 ☐

pH 7 ☐

pH 8 ☐

pH 9 ☐

[1 mark]

03.8 Explain your answer to 03.7

....

....

....

[2 marks]

04 Plant and animal cells have different characteristics.

04.1 Draw **one** line from each cell characteristic to the correct type of cell.

Cell characteristic

Plant cell		Animal cell
	Plasma membrane only, no cell wall	
	Carbohydrate stored as glycogen	
	Chloroplasts	
	Large vacuole	

[3 marks]

04.2 When using a microscope, live cells can be mounted in a drop of water on a microscope slide.

They are then covered using a transparent coverslip.

Which of the following is a reason for using a coverslip?

Tick **one** box.

To kill the specimen ☐

To keep the specimen flat ☐

To preserve the specimen ☐

To trap air in the specimen ☐

[1 mark]

Question 4 continues on the next page

04.3 Which stain is used to add colour and contrast to plant cells to look at them under the microscope?

Tick **one** box.

Hydrogen peroxide ☐

Iodine solution ☐

Methylene blue ☐

Potassium dichromate ☐

[1 mark]

04.4 Look at **Figure 4.1**

The diagrams are **not** to scale.

Figure 4.1

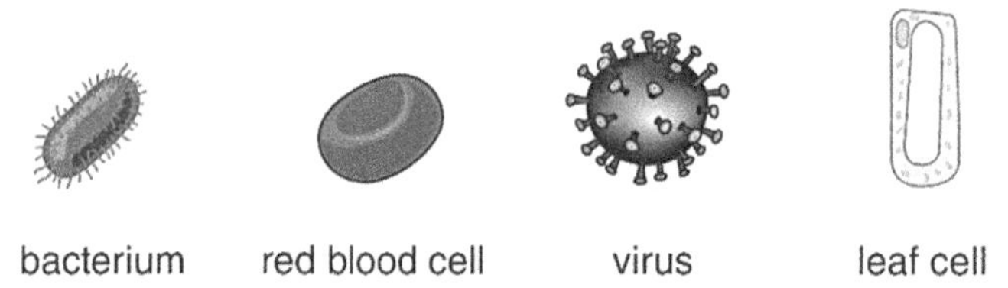

bacterium   red blood cell   virus   leaf cell

Write the cells and virus in order of their size, from the smallest to the largest.

Smallest ....

....

....

Largest .... **[1 mark]**

04.5 **Figure 4.2** shows a low-power micrograph of a plant root. The root is approximately 2 mm in diameter just below the meristem.

Figure 4.2

Draw a diagram of the plant root.

Label the meristem on your diagram.

Draw an appropriate scale bar on your diagram.

[4 marks]

Turn over >

05 An estimated 42% of cancer cases each year in the UK are linked to lifestyle choices.

Look at **Figure 5.1**

Figure 5.1

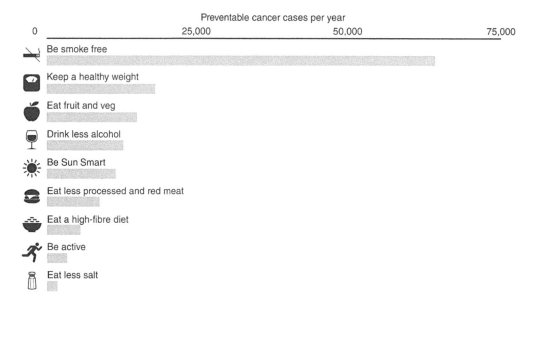

05.1 How many preventable cancers were related to smoking?

....

[1 mark]

05.2 Compare the numbers of preventable cancers related to **being active** with those related to **drinking less alcohol.**

....

....

[2 marks]

05.3 The most common types of cancers are different for men compared with women.

Suggest a reason for this.

[1 mark]

05.4 Use the data in **Figure 5.1** to describe a healthy diet to reduce the risk of developing cancer.

[2 marks]

05.5 Tobacco is by far the most common cause of cancer in the UK.

What type of cancer is commonly linked with tobacco smoking?

[1 mark]

05.6 Describe the difference between a benign tumour and a malignant tumour.

Benign tumour:

[1 mark]

Malignant tumour:

[2 marks]

Turn over >

06 A vaccination introduces a small quantity of dead pathogen into the body to protect us from disease.

A new vaccination has been developed against the pathogen Lumpius.

The Lumpius vaccine is being tested by a pharmaceutical company, which has recruited 10 000 volunteers.

Figure 6.1 shows the body's response to the vaccination and later to infection by Lumpius.

Figure 6.1

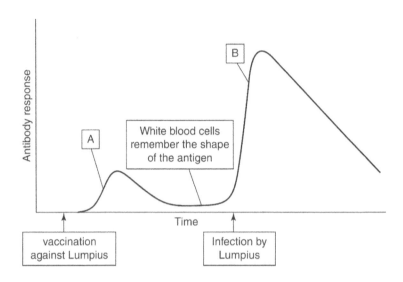

06.1 Explain why antibodies are being produced at A.

....

....

.... **[1 mark]**

06.2 Why is the antibody response much bigger at B compared with A?

....

....

.... **[2 marks]**

06.3 Explain why the pharmaceutical company thinks that the vaccine is effective.

_____

_____

_____ **[2 marks]**

06.4 At what stage of development is the vaccine?

Tick **one** box.

Animal testing ☐

Laboratory testing ☐

Clinical trial ☐

Pre-clinical trial ☐

[1 mark]

Give a reason for your answer.

_____ **[1 mark]**

06.4 Different types of disease may interact.

Complete the following sentences:

* Defects in the immune system mean that an individual is more

    likely to suffer from _____ .

* Immune reactions initially caused by a pathogen can trigger

    _____ . **[2 marks]**

07 Jane has set up equipment to investigate the rate of photosynthesis in an aquatic plant.

She uses a lamp as a light source.

Figure 7.1

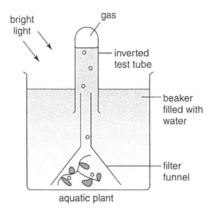

07.1 Look at **Figure 7.1**

What is the name of the gas collecting in the test tube?

_____ **[1 mark]**

07.2 How can Jane measure the amount of gas produced?

_____

_____ **[2 marks]**

07.3 Jane could have measured the amount of gas more accurately.

What piece of equipment would Jane need to use to do this?

_____ **[1 mark]**

07.4 For her investigation, Jane will need to:

- know how far the lamp is from the apparatus

- know how much gas is produced

- keep the water at a constant temperature.

Name **two** other pieces of equipment that Jane will need.

_____

_____ **[2 marks]**

07.5 Explain how Jane should carry out her investigation.

_____

_____

_____

_____

_____

_____

_____

_____

_____

_____ **[6 marks]**

07.6 Jane wants a pond in her garden to keep fish.

Explain why she should dig her pond in a sunny part of the garden.

_____

_____ **[2 marks]**

Turn over >

08 During exercise the human body reacts to the increased demand for energy.

Look at **Figure 8.1**

Changes are happening to this jogger as he runs.

Figure 8.1

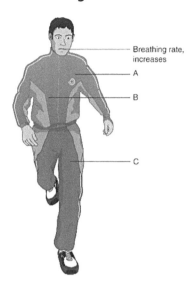

08.1 What is happening at A?

_____

_____ **[2 marks]**

08.2 What is happening at B?

_____

_____ **[2 marks]**

08.3 What is happening at C?

_____

_____ **[2 marks]**

08.4 What type of respiration occurs when there is not enough oxygen supplied to the muscles?

_____ **[1 mark]**

08.5 Which acid builds up in the muscles during hard exercise?

Tick **one** box.

Acetic acid ☐

Amino acid ☐

Citric acid ☐

Lactic acid ☐

[1 mark]

08.6 **Figure 8.2** shows the effects of exercise on the heart rates of two people.

Figure 8.2

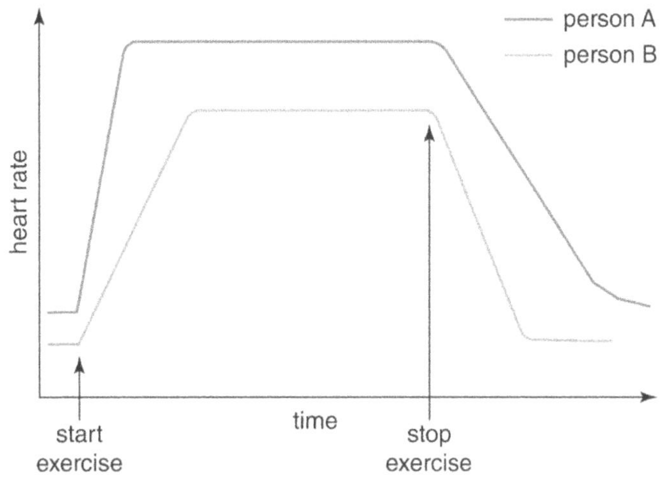

Which person is fitter?

Tick **one** box.

Person A ☐

Person B ☐

[1 mark]

08.7 Give **two** reasons for your answer.
Use the shape of the graph to help you.

_____

_____

_____

_____

[2 marks]

Turn over >

09   **Figure 9.1** shows part of a plant cell under a microscope.

Figure 9.1

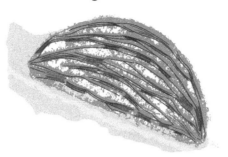

09.1 What is the name of this structure?

Tick **one** box.

Chloroplast ☐

Cytoplasm ☐

Nucleus ☐

Vacuole ☐   **[1 mark]**

09.2 During photosynthesis, plants harness the Sun's energy and make food.

Describe photosynthesis, the factors that affect it and how plants use the products.

....

....

....

....

....

....

....

....

....

                                                                                              [6 marks]

09.3 The effect of a range of salt concentrations on the mass of identical potato cylinders was investigated.

What are the independent and dependent variables in this investigation?

Independent variable:

.... **[1 mark]**

Dependent variable:

....

.... **[1 mark]**

Turn over >

10   **Figure 10.1** shows two different types of fox.

Fennec foxes live in hot desert areas.

Arctic foxes live cold regions.

Figure 10.1

| Fennec fox | Arctic fox |

Sue wants to compare the surface area of the ears of these foxes.

Their ears are not regular shapes.

To measure the surface areas of the ears, Sue:

- takes measurements of the left ear of a fox

- draws the shape of the ear onto graph paper

- uses the graph paper to help her find the surface
  area of the ear.

Figure 10.2 shows the measurements of the left ear of an Arctic fox drawn on graph paper.

Each large square is 1 cm x 1 cm

The diagram is **not** to scale.

Figure 10.2

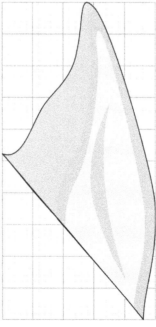

10.1 What is the surface area of one side of the Arctic fox's ear?

Surface area _____

Units _____ **[2 marks]**

10.2 The surface area of one side of the fennec fox's ear is 228 cm^2

Calculate how much bigger the fennec fox's ear is, when compared with the Arctic fox's ear.

Write this as a percentage.

Give your answer using an appropriate number of significant figures.

Size of fennec fox's ear = 228 cm^2

Size of Arctic fox's ear = _____ (your answer to 10.1 from above)

_____

_____

_____

_____

The fennec fox's ear is bigger by: _____ %   **[3 marks]**

10.3 Suggest a reason why fennec foxes may have **larger** ears than Arctic foxes.

_____

_____

_____

_____ **[2 marks]**

END OF QUESTIONS

BLANK PAGE

Collins

AQA
GCSE

Biology

F

SET B – Paper 2 Foundation Tier

Author: Kath Skillern

Materials

Time allowed: 1 hour 45 minutes

For this paper you must have:

- a ruler
- a calculator.

Instructions

- Answer **all** questions in the spaces provided.
- Do all rough work in this book. Cross through any work you do not want to be marked.

Information

- There are 100 marks available on this paper.
- The marks for questions are shown in brackets.
- You are expected to use a calculator where appropriate.
- You are reminded of the need for good English and clear presentation in your answers.
- When answering questions 04.6 and 06.5 you need to make sure that your answer:
  - is clear, logical, sensibly structured
  - fully meets the requirements of the question
  - shows that each separate point or step supports the overall answer.

Advice

- In all calculations, show clearly how you work out your answer.

Name: ....

01 An ecosystem is the interaction of a community of living organisms with the non-living parts of their environment.

01.1 How is the **non-living** part of the environment described?

Tick **one** box.

Abiotic   ☐

Biotic   ☐

Dead   ☐

Habitat   ☐   **[1 mark]**

01.2 Name **two** resources that **plants** compete for.

1. ....

2. .... **[2 marks]**

01.3 Name **two** resources that **animals** compete for.

1. ....

2. .... **[2 marks]**

01.4 Within a community each species depends on other species to help it survive.

If one species is removed it can affect the whole community.

How is this described?

Tick **one** box.

Interaction   ☐

Interdependence   ☐

Ecosystem   ☐

Environment   ☐   **[1 mark]**

01.5 Explain the term 'a stable community'.

....

....

.... [2 marks]

01.6 Biological material eventually dies and decays.

What does **anaerobic** decay produce?

Tick **one** box.

Carbon dioxide ☐

Ethane ☐

Lactic acid ☐

Methane ☐ [1 mark]

01.7 Which **two** materials do microorganisms cycle through an ecosystem?

Tick **two** boxes.

Carbon dioxide ☐

Compost ☐

Mineral ions ☐

Oxygen ☐ [2 marks]

Turn over >

02   The human body reacts to changes by coordinating a **nervous** response or a **hormonal** response.

02.1 Draw a line from each response description to **either** the nervous system **or** the hormonal system.

System	Response description	System
	Fast acting	
	Slow acting	
	Acts for short time	
	Acts for long time	
Nervous system		Hormonal system
	Chemical	
	Electrical	
	Acts in a specific area	
	Acts more generally	

[4 marks]

02.2 In a scientific study, called **Scientific Study A**, reaction times were investigated after four volunteers had drunk alcohol.

A small can of beer contains about one unit of alcohol.

The results are shown in **Table 2.1**

Table 2.1

Volunteer		Reaction time in milliseconds (ms)				
	Units of alcohol	0.5	1.5	3.0	4.5	6.0
A		34	45	59	71	85
B		35	47	62	75	87
C		32	46	64	72	83
D		30	42	59	70	81
Mean		33	45	61	72	

Calculate the mean reaction time of the volunteers after 6.0 units of alcohol.

Mean reaction time after 6.0 units of alcohol = _____ **[3 marks]**

02.3 Use the results in **Table 2.1** to **describe** how alcohol affects reaction time.

[2 marks]

02.4 In **Scientific Study B**, a test was carried out on 2000 people of all ages.

Comment on the repeatability of **Scientific Studies A and B**.

Turn over >

03   Type 2 diabetes is a serious condition.

In Type 2 diabetes the body's cells no longer respond as effectively to control glucose concentration in the blood.

Look at **Table 3.1**

Table 3.1

Year	Proportion (%) of the population who have Type 2 diabetes	Mean body mass in kg
1990	4.9	72.5
1991	5.0	73.0
1992	5.4	73.7
1993	4.7	74.0
1994	5.3	74.6
1995	5.5	75.0
1996	5.4	74.8
1997	6.2	75.3
1998	6.5	76.0
1999	6.9	76.6
2000	7.3	77.2

03.1 Use the data in **Table 3.1** to plot a graph to show the effect of body mass on the percentage of the population who have Type 2 diabetes.

You do not need to use the Year column in **Table 3.1**.

Make sure to:

- choose an appropriate scale
- label both axes
- plot all points to show the pattern of results.

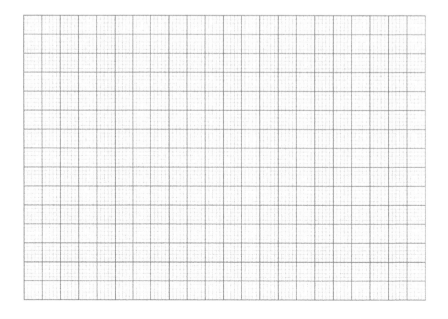

[4 marks]

03.2 Describe the relationship between the mean body mass of the population and the percentage of people who have Type 2 diabetes.

....

....

[1 mark]

03.3 Water moves around the body, and into and out of it, continuously.

Complete the sentences below.

When you **exhale**…

Tick **one** box.

A	water, ions and urea leave the body via the skin	
B	water, ions and urea are removed via the kidneys	
C	water leaves the body via the lungs	

[1 mark]

When you **sweat**…

Tick **one** box.

A	water, ions and urea leave the body via the skin	
B	water, ions and urea are removed via the kidneys	
C	water leaves the body via the lungs	

[1 mark]

When you **urinate**…

Tick **one** box.

A	water, ions and urea leave the body via the skin	
B	water, ions and urea are removed via the kidneys	
C	water leaves the body via the lungs	

[1 mark]

Question 3 continues on the next page

03.4 Which organ regulates water loss?

Tick **one** box.

Bladder ☐

Kidney ☐

Lung ☐

Skin ☐ [1 mark]

03.5 Hormones control reproduction:

- Follicle stimulating hormone (FSH) causes maturation of an egg in the ovary.

- Oestrogen and progesterone are involved in maintaining the uterus lining.

Use this information to explain how **one hormonal** method of contraception works.

....

....

.... [2 marks]

04   Evolutionary trees are used by scientists to show how organisms are related.

Figure 4.1 shows an evolutionary tree.

The numbers on the branches of the evolutionary tree are the number of 'million years ago'.

Figure 4.1

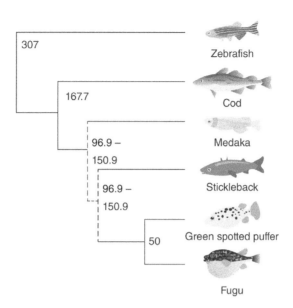

04.1 Which fish is the most **distantly** related to the others?

Tick **one** box.

Cod   ☐

Fugu   ☐

Green spotted puffer   ☐

Medaka   ☐

Stickleback   ☐

Zebrafish   ☐   [1 mark]

Question 4 continues on the next page

04.2 Which **two** fishes are most **closely** related?

Tick **two** boxes.

Cod ☐

Fugu ☐

Green spotted puffer ☐

Medaka ☐

Stickleback ☐

Zebrafish ☐ [1 mark]

04.3 How long ago did the cod split from medaka and stickleback?

_____ [1 mark]

04.4 Suggest why there is only a **dotted** line between medaka and stickleback.

_____

_____ [1 mark]

04.5 Name **one** type of evidence that helps scientists construct evolutionary trees.

_____ [1 mark]

04.6 Describe the steps which may have given rise to medaka and stickleback becoming different species.

_____

_____

_____

_____

_____

_____

_____

_____

_____

_____

_____

_____

_____

_____

_____

[6 marks]

Turn over >

05   **Figure 5.1** shows a section through a human brain.

Figure 5.1

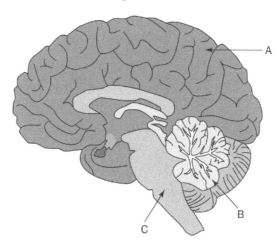

05.1 What is the area labelled **A** on **Figure 5.1**?

Tick **one** box.

Cerebellum   ☐

Cerebral cortex   ☐

Medusa   ☐

Pituitary   ☐   **[1 mark]**

05.2 What is the area labelled **B** on **Figure 5.1**?

Tick **one** box.

Cerebellum   ☐

Cerebral cortex   ☐

Hypothalamus   ☐

Medulla   ☐   **[1 mark]**

05.3 What is the area labelled **C** on **Figure 5.1**?

Tick **one** box.

Medulla ☐

Medusa ☐

Optic nerve ☐

Spinal column ☐

[1 mark]

05.4 The brain has many functions, including highly complex functions and unconscious, automatic functions.

What is the function of area **A**, area **B** and area **C**?

Give **one** example for each.

Area A

Function: ....

Example: ....

Area B

Function: ....

Example: ....

Area C

Function: ....

Example: .... **[6 marks]**

Question 5 continues on the next page

05.5 **Figure 5.2** shows the brain weight and body mass of animals.

Figure 5.2

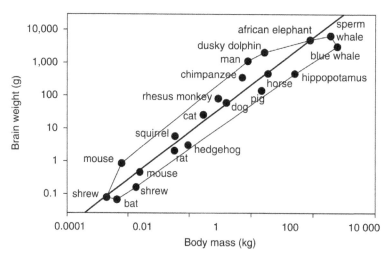

Describe the relationship between the size of an animal and the size of its brain.

....

....

[1 mark]

05.6 Suggest **one** reason for this relationship.

....

....

[1 mark]

06 Some of the characteristics of living things are controlled by a single gene, such as fur colour in mice.

Figure 6.1 shows the alleles for fur colour for three mice.

Figure 6.1

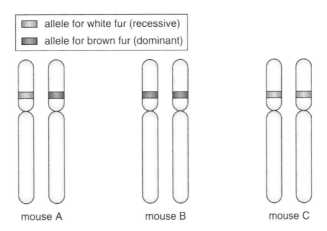

06.1 How are the alleles of Mouse A described?

Tick **one** box.

Dominant ☐

Heterozygous ☐

Homozygous ☐

Phenotype ☐   [1 mark]

06.2 Which mouse or mice have brown fur?

Tick **one** box.

Mouse B only ☐

Mice A and B ☐

Mouse A only ☐

Mice A and C ☐   [1 mark]

Question 6 continues on the next page

06.3 If Mouse B and Mouse C were to breed, what colour fur would their offspring have?

_____ **[1 mark]**

06.4 Explain your answer to 06.3

_____

_____

_____

_____

[3 marks]

06.5 The DNA molecule is a polymer, that contains four different bases.

Figure 6.2 shows the structure of DNA.

Figure 6.2

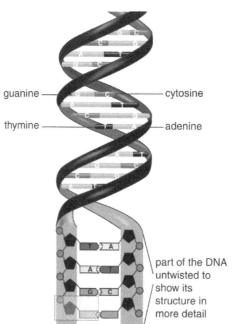

Describe the structure and function of DNA.

In your answer describe where DNA is found.

Use **Figure 6.2** to help you.

[6 marks]

07   **Figure 7.1** shows five closely related species of fish, with their diets and habitats.

Figure 7.1

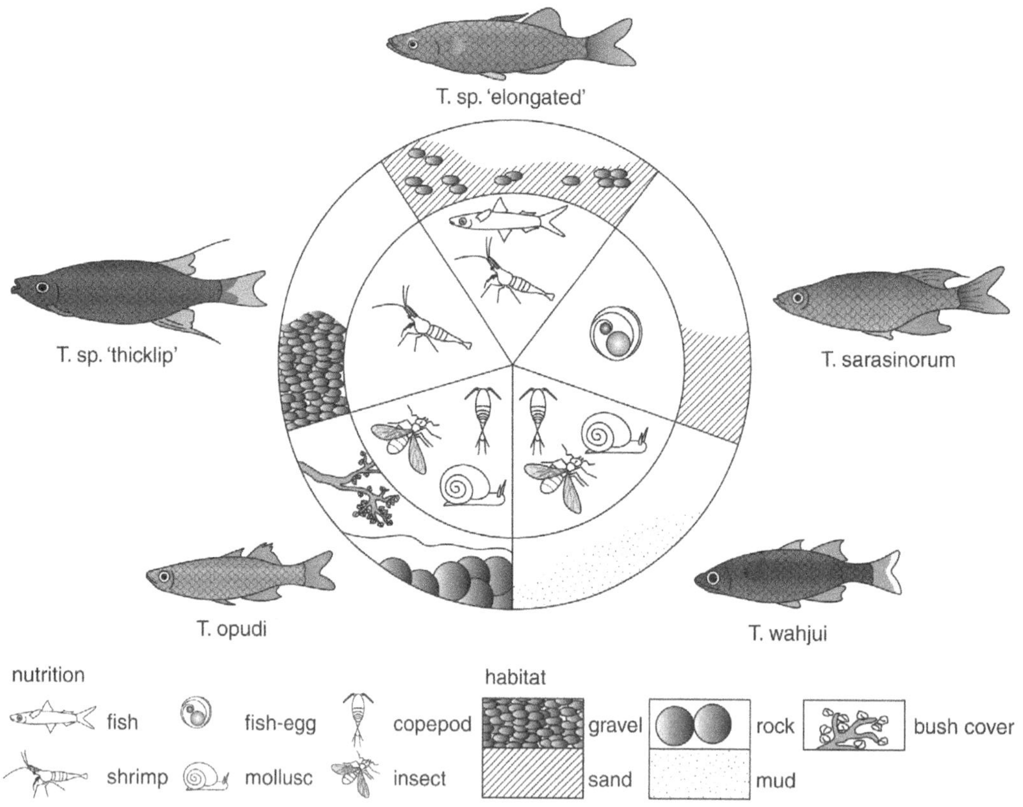

07.1   The copepods in this community are primary consumers.

Suggest what their diet may consist of.

_____

[1 mark]

07.2 In one year, there was a huge increase in the numbers of *T. sarasinorum*.

How would this affect the numbers of 'thicklip'?

Explain your answer.

[3 marks]

07.3 Explain why *T. opudi* and *T. wahjui* are **not** competitors, even though they have similar diets.

[2 marks]

07.4 Name a source of pollution that could affect the fish.

[1 mark]

07.5 Explain why pyramids of biomass are rarely higher than four organisms.

[3 marks]

Turn over >

08 In the year 2000, a litter of piglets was produced by cloning.

One of the piglets born was called Millie.

Figure 8.1 shows the cloning of Millie the piglet.

Figure 8.1

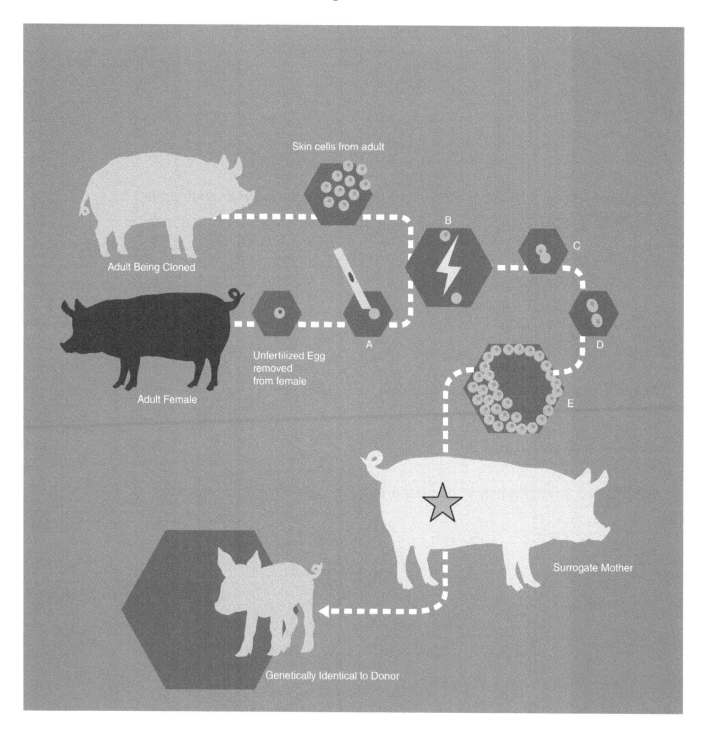

08.1 Look at **Figure 8.1**

Suggest labels to describe the cloning process at points **A**, **B**, **C**, **D** and **E**.

A ....

B ....

C ....

D ....

E .... **[5 marks]**

08.2 In the year 2001, a kitten called Copy Cat was produced by cloning.

Copy Cat was genetically identical to the cloned cat, but the patterns on her fur were different.

Suggest a reason for this.

.... **[1 mark]**

08.3 Some organisms naturally produce clones by **asexual** reproduction.

Name an organism that naturally produces clones.

.... **[1 mark]**

Question 8 continues on the next page

08.4 Give **two** advantages of asexual reproduction.

....

....

....

....

[2 marks]

08.5 A gardener has been breeding roses in her garden.

She selects the roses with the biggest blossoms and most fragrant flowers to breed together, and pollinates them herself.

How is the gardener's method of breeding described?

....

[1 mark]

08.6 A farmer's cabbages suffer from white fly.

The farmer asks a local plant laboratory to create for him a resistant breed of cabbage.

How is the farmer's method of breeding described?

....

[1 mark]

08.7 Describe the differences between the gardener's and the farmer's approaches to improving their plants.

....

....

....

....

[2 marks]

09.1 Explain the difference between **population size** and **population density**.

....

....

....

[2 marks]

09.2 Mr Green needs to assess the population of plantain on a 10 m wide path in a national park.

Figure 9.1 shows broadleaf plantain, which is a tough plant often found on footpaths.

Figure 9.1

Mr Green has a 25 cm² wire quadrat and a measuring tape.

He places the tape across the path, including the dense verges either side of the path.

What is the name of this line?

.... [1 mark]

Question 9 continues on the next page

09.3 Mr Green places the quadrat at the end of the line, on the verge.

He counts the number of whole plants in the quadrat and records the number.

How should Mr Green decide where to place the **next** quadrat along the line?

[2 marks]

09.4 Mr Green samples along the line, until he reaches the other end.

The whole path is 500 m long.

Describe the steps Mr Green should follow so that he has statistical evidence for the distribution of plantain **along the length of the path**.

[3 marks]

09.5 Explain why there are likely to be more plantains in the **middle** of the path than at the edges.

[2 marks]

END OF QUESTIONS

Answers

Set A – Paper 1

Question	Answer(s)	Extra info	Mark(s)	AO/Spec ref.
01.1	B any **one** from: • axon / long fibre • nerve endings • cell body • sheath		1 1	AO1 4.1.1.3
01.2	C projection / hair	allow is the only plant cell or point that implies this e.g. it is the only one with a cell wall / large vacuole	1 1	AO1 4.1.1.3
01.3	A tail	allow can swim	1 1	AO1 4.1.1.3
01.4	C any **one** from: • has a cell wall • has a large vacuole	allow is a root hair cell	1 1	AO1 4.1.1.2
02.1	oxygen		1	AO1 4.4.1.1
02.2	palisade mesophyll		1	AO1 4.2.3.1
02.3	$C_6H_{12}O_6$		1	AO1 4.4.1.1
02.4	amino acids – protein synthesis cellulose – strengthen cell walls starch – food storage all three correct for **2 marks** one or two correct for **1 mark**	each extra line negates a mark	2	AO1 4.4.1.3
02.5	phloem translocation	in this order only	1 1	AO1 4.2.3.2
02.6	midday it is warmer the light is brighter	allow the stomata are fully open	1 1 1	AO2/ AO3 4.4.1.2

Question	Answer(s)	Extra info	Mark(s)	AO/Spec ref.
03.1	plasma – carry dissolved food and other substances around the body platelets – form blood clots white blood cells – protect the body against infection all three correct for **2 marks** one or two correct for **1 mark**	each extra line negates a mark	2	AO1 4.2.2.3
03.2	more likely to become infected **or** less able to defend against pathogens		1	AO2 4.3.1.6
03.3	artery – thick, elastic wall small lumen capillary – wall is one cell thick vein – thin wall large lumen with valves all three correct for **2 marks** one or two correct for **1 mark**	each extra line negates a mark	2	AO1 4.2.2.2
03.4	less oxygen / glucose gets to heart muscle heart muscle respires less / works less efficiently		1 1	AO1/ AO2 4.2.2.4 4.4.2.1
03.5	artificial heart this will keep the patient alive until donor heart available		1 1	AO3 4.2.2.4
04.1	blocks oxygen / air from the water **or** stops larva / pupa breathing **or** prevents mosquitoes laying eggs **or** hampers adult emerging reduces risk of being bitten		1 1	AO2 4.3.1.5
04.2	they are unlikely to bite someone with malaria so they do not carry / transmit *Plasmodium* (if they bite someone else)		1 1	AO3 4.3.1.5

Question	Answer(s)	Extra info	Mark(s)	AO/Spec ref.
04.3	measles – viral rose black spot – fungal salmonella food poisoning – bacterial all three correct for **2 marks** one or two correct for **1 mark**	each extra line negates a mark	2	**AO1** 4.3.1.2 4.3.1.3 4.3.1.4
04.4	it has a nucleus it does not have a cell wall	allow it does not have plasmids allow DNA is not in a loop allow it does not have a (slime) capsule allow it does not have flagella	1 1	**AO2** 4.1.1.1
05.1	aspirin – willow tree digitalis – foxglove plant penicillin – *Penicillium* mould all three correct for **2 marks** one or two correct for **1 mark**	each extra line negates a mark	2	**AO1** 4.3.1.9
05.2	any **two** from: • it's easier / quicker • it's cheaper • can produce in greater quantities		2	**AO2** 4.3.1.9
05.3	**Level 2:** A detailed and coherent argument is given, describing the effect of aspirin upon the risk of dying from cancer.		3–4	**AO3** 4.2.2.5
	Level 1: Discrete relevant points are made, although the arguments may not be clear.		1–2	

Question	Answer(s)	Extra info	Mark(s)	AO/Spec ref.
	No relevant content		0	
	Indicative content • starting to take aspirin up to 2 years (before death) has no effect on risk of dying from cancer / there is no difference between taking aspirin and taking a placebo • starting to take aspirin for more than 2 years (before death) reduces risk of dying from cancer / compared with a placebo • as time from starting to take aspirin before death increases, aspirin has a greater effect reducing risk of dying from cancer / compared with a placebo			
06.1	fermentation		1	**AO1** 4.4.2.1
06.2	keep out oxygen so yeast does anaerobic respiration **or** so yeast cannot use aerobic respiration, which gives different products		1 1	**AO2** 4.4.2.1
06.3	to allow carbon dioxide to escape otherwise pressure will build up		1 1	**AO2** 4.4.2.1
06.4	glucose → lactic acid	all correct for **2 marks** allow **1** mark if glucose shown as reactant **or** lactic acid shown as product deduct mark for each additional incorrect reactant or product (e.g. oxygen, carbon dioxide) allow correct symbols in place of glucose or lactic acid	2	**AO1** 4.4.2.1
06.5	any **one** from: • lactic acid causes fatigue / aches • anaerobic respiration transfers less energy than aerobic respiration		1	**AO2** 4.4.2.1 4.4.2.2
07.1	8		1	**AO2** 4.1.1.6

Question	Answer(s)	Extra info	Mark(s)	AO/Spec ref.
07.2	(step 1:) to sterilise the loop / kill any unwanted microorganisms		1	**AO1** 4.1.1.6
	(step 2:) to avoid killing bacteria from the culture		1	
	(step 8:) to prevent water dropping on to the colonies / prevent any airborne microorganisms falling onto the agar		1	
	(step 9:) warm enough to encourage growth / not warm enough to **encourage** growth of harmful pathogens / not warm enough to kill the bacteria		1	
07.3	C		1	AO3 **4.1.1.6**
	it has the largest area with no bacteria growing / largest zone of inhibition		1	
07.4	to work out a mean / average		1	AO2 4.1.1.6
	the zones are not perfect circles		1	
08.1	(spines) deter animals		1	AO2 4.3.3.2
	so plant is not eaten		1	
	(waxy coating) provides a barrier against microorganisms **OR** heat to help survive in the desert		1 1	
08.2	any **two** from: • yellow / pale green (in colour) • (magnesium is) needed to make chlorophyll • cannot photosynthesise as much		2	AO2 4.3.3.1
09.1	malignant	in this order only	1	AO1 4.2.2.7
	benign		1	
09.2	allow air to move in and out of lungs		1	AO1 4.2.2.2
09.3	undifferentiated / unspecialised cells		1	AO1 4.1.2.3
	that can develop into other types of cell		1	
09.4	ethical / religious objection to using human stem cells	ignore unqualified reference to ethical / religious objection allow other specific ethical / religious objection	1	AO1 4.1.2.3
09.5	(stem cells / new cells) not attacked by patient's immune system / white blood cells	allow no ethical / religious objections	1	AO2 4.3.1.6

Question	Answer(s)	Extra info	Mark(s)	AO/Spec ref.
10.1	(medicines like aspirin) are painkillers / treat the symptoms		1	AO2 4.3.1.8
	(antibiotics) do not kill viruses		1	
10.2	any **two** from: • test for toxicity / safety • test for efficacy / effectiveness • test to find best dose		2	AO1 4.3.1.9
10.3	**Level 2:** A detailed and coherent argument is given, which explains why placebos should be used with healthy volunteers but not ill patients.		3–4	AO3 4.3.1.9
	Level 1: Discrete relevant points are made, although the arguments may not be clear.		1–2	
	No relevant content		0	
	Indicative content • a placebo is a treatment that does not contain the (active) medicine / drug • placebos are used with a control group / to compare with the group taking the medicine / drug • placebos can be used with healthy volunteers • placebos should not be used with ill patients • if ill patients took placebos then would not be getting any treatment • trials involving ill patients should use currently available medicines / drugs for the control group			
10.4	to avoid bias	allow so that neither doctors or participants know who has received the (active) medicine / drug (until the trial is completed)	1	AO2 4.3.1.9
11.1	in order: virus, red blood cell, ant, acorn all correct for **2** marks allow **1** mark if three are in the correct order		2	AO2 4.1.1.1
11.2	60 mm = 60 000 μm magnification = 60 000 ÷ 12 = 5000 **OR** if converted to $$mm = \frac{60 \times 10^3}{12 \times 10^{-6}}$$ = 5000	allow 5000 with no working shown for **3** marks allow equivalent marking points if 12 μm is converted to 0.012 mm	1 1 1	AO2 4.1.1.5

Question	Answer(s)	Extra info	Mark(s)	AO/Spec ref.
11.3	to make the structures more visible		1	AO1 4.1.1.2
	to have a large field of view / to see the layout of cells / easier to locate cells		1	
12.1	all points correctly plotted 2 marks **but** three or four points correctly plotted 1 mark	allow ± half a small square	2	AO2/AO3 4.2.3.2
	anomalous result (25 mm) circled		1	
	straight line of best fit through all points except anomalous result		1	
12.2	as water evaporated / transpired from the leaves, water was pulled through the capillary tube (moving the air bubble)		1	AO2 4.2.3.2
12.3	**Level 3:** A coherent method is described with relevant detail, which demonstrates a broad understanding of the relevant scientific techniques and procedures. The steps in the method are logically ordered. The method would lead to the collection of valid results.		5–6	AO3 4.2.3.2
	Level 2: The bulk of a method is described with mostly relevant detail, which demonstrates a reasonable understanding of the relevant techniques and procedures. The method may not be in a completely logical sequence and may be missing some detail.		3–4	
	Level 1: Discrete relevant points are made which demonstrate some understanding of the relevant scientific techniques and procedures. They may lack a logical structure and would not lead to the production of valid results.		1–2	
	No relevant content		0	
	Indicative content • independent variable is air movement • air movement varied by altering the speed of the fan / distance of fan from plant using measuring equipment • dependent variable is distance bubble moves in a given time or time for bubble to move a given distance • control variables include: same plant, temperature, light intensity, humidity • repeat readings and calculate means			

Set A – Paper 2

Question	Answer(s)	Extra info	Mark(s)	AO/Spec ref.
01.1	blood vessels dilate (get wider)		1	AO1 4.5.2.4
	sweat is produced		1	
01.2	brain	in this order only	1	AO1 4.5.2.4
	blood		1	
01.3	*see table below*		2	AO1 4.5.3.3

Process	Increases water in the body	Decreases water in the body
Breathing		✓
Eating	✓	
Sweating		✓
Urinating		✓

all four rows correct for **2 marks**

two or three rows correct for **1 mark**

Question	Answer(s)	Extra info	Mark(s)	AO/Spec ref.
01.4	homeostasis		1	AO1 4.5.1
02.1	**X** = pituitary **Y** = pancreas **Z** = adrenal		1 1 1	AO1 4.5.3.1
02.2	in the blood (system)		1	AO1 4.5.3.1
02.3	insulin – pancreas oestrogen – ovary testosterone – testis all three correct for **2 marks** one or two correct for **1 mark**	each extra line negates a mark	2	AO1 4.5.3.2 4.5.3.4
02.4	(type 1) diabetes		1	AO1 4.5.3.2
03.1	Arctic willow / grass		1	AO2 4.7.2.1
03.2	Arctic fox / snowy owl		1	AO2 4.7.2.1
03.3	the number would increase		1	AO3 4.7.1.1
	they have more food / Arctic hares to eat **or** there is less competition for food (with the Arctic foxes)		1	
03.4	community		1	AO1 4.7.11
03.5	mates		1	AO1 4.7.1.3

Question	Answer(s)	Extra info	Mark(s)	AO/Spec ref.
03.6	any **one** adaptation with corresponding explanation: sharp / pointed teeth; to catch prey sharp / pointed claws; to catch prey eyes at front of head; binocular vision / judge distance white fur; camouflage	only award explanation mark if it matches with the adaptation	2	**AO2** 4.7.1.4
03.7	any **one** adaptation with corresponding explanation: eyes at side of head; wide field of view large ears; hear predators white fur; camouflage long legs; escape from predators	only award explanation mark if it matches with the adaptation	2	**AO2** 4.7.1.4
04.1	FSH – causes eggs to mature LH – stimulates the release of eggs Progesterone – maintains uterus lining all three correct for **2 marks** one or two correct for **1 mark**	each extra line negates a mark	2	**AO1** 4.5.3.4
04.2	<table><tr><td>Type of cell</td><td>Number of chromosomes in cell</td></tr><tr><td>Sperm</td><td>23</td></tr><tr><td>Egg</td><td>23</td></tr><tr><td>Fertilised egg</td><td>46</td></tr><tr><td>Embryo</td><td>46</td></tr></table>all three correct for **2 marks** one or two correct for **1 mark**		2	**AO2** 4.6.1.2
04.3	differentiation		1	**AO1** 4.6.1.2

Question	Answer(s)	Extra info	Mark(s)	AO/Spec ref.
04.4	diaphragm – prevents sperm reaching egg intrauterine device (IUD) – prevents fertilised egg implanting oral contraceptive – prevents eggs maturing spermicide – kills sperm all four correct for **3 marks** two or three correct for **2 marks** one correct for **1 mark**	each extra line negates a mark	3	**AO1** 4.5.3.5
05.1	100 – 13 – 4 – 9 – 58 = 16 (%)	allow 16 (%) with no working shown for **2 marks**	1 1	**AO2** 4.7.3.5
05.2	emissions from power stations burning fossil fuels / oil / coal / (natural) gas		1 1	**AO1** 4.7.2.2
05.3	industrial sector – no mark on own jet fuel produces 20% of 58% = 12%	allow industrial sector because jet fuel produces 12 (%) **1 mark**	1 1	**AO2** 4.7.3.5
05.4	global warming	allow increased greenhouse effect ignore greenhouse effect allow description of consequences of global warming, e.g. flooding / drought / famine / climate change	1	**AO1** 4.7.3.5
05.5	photosynthesis		1	**AO1** 4.7.2.2
06.1	scar		1	**AO2** 4.6.2.1
06.2	DNA double helix chromosome	in this order only	1 1 1	**AO1** 4.6.1.4

Question	Answer(s)	Extra info	Mark(s)	AO/Spec ref.
06.3	<table><tr><td></td><td>A</td><td>a</td></tr><tr><td>A</td><td>AA</td><td>Aa</td></tr><tr><td>a</td><td>Aa</td><td>aa</td></tr></table> all three correct for **2** marks / one or two correct for **1** mark		2	AO2 4.6.1.6
06.4	wet (earwax)		1	AO2 4.6.1.6
06.5	heterozygous		1	AO2 4.6.1.6
07.1	(intensively reared hens) use less energy / biomass moving so more energy / biomass is used for egg production		1 1	AO1 4.7.4.3 4.7.5.2
07.2	(cost more because) fewer eggs are produced so farmers need to charge more to maintain income (people pay more because) they have ethical objections to intensive farming, e.g. concerns about animal welfare		1 1	AO3 4.7.5.2
07.3	climate change – less water available for crops increasing birth rate – more people need food pests – eat or damage crops all three correct for **2** marks one or two correct for **1** mark	each extra line negates a mark	2	AO2 4.7.5.1
07.4	quotas: limit number that can be caught / enough are left to breed and maintain population net size: smaller nets catch fewer fish / larger hole sizes allow smaller fish to escape and breed		1 1	AO2 4.7.5.3
08.1	select a male and female with more meat than others breed these together from their offspring select those with most meat use these for breeding repeat over many generations		1 1 1 1 1	AO1 4.6.2.3
08.2	large udder to produce more milk **OR** smaller horns to avoid harm to farmer / so energy can be used for meat/ milk production instead		2	AO2 4.6.2.3

Question	Answer(s)	Extra info	Mark(s)	AO/Spec ref.
08.3	genetic engineering		1	AO1 4.6.2.4
09.1	so a large number of clones can be produced (and each needs its own mother)		1	AO2 4.6.2.5
09.2	other offspring		1	AO2 4.6.2.5
09.3	**Level 2:** A detailed and coherent argument is given, which explains at least one advantage and one disadvantage of growing from cuttings.		3–4	AO1/AO2 4.6.1.1 4.6.1.3 4.6.2.5
	Level 1: Discrete relevant points are made, although the arguments may not be clear.		1–2	
	No relevant content		0	
	Advantages • the new plants will have the same characteristics as the parents, so you know what characteristics the new plants will have • it's quicker to grow new plants from cuttings **Disadvantages** • the new plants will have the same characteristics as the parents, so there will be no new varieties • the new plants will have the same characteristics as the parents, so if the original plant is susceptible to a disease / pest then so will the offspring • (usually) fewer new plants produced from each parent plant (compared with growing from seeds)			
10.1	direction of light make sure light comes from all directions / dish is equally lit from all directions because seedlings will also respond to the direction of light / seedlings are phototropic		1 1 1	AO2 4.5.4.1
10.2	to make sure results are repeatable / to make sure result is not anomalous		1	AO2 4.5.4.1
10.3	auxin collected on lower side of shoot increased growth / elongation on lower side (causes upward growth)		1 1	AO2 4.5.4.1

Question	Answer(s)	Extra info	Mark(s)	AO/Spec ref.
10.4	seedlings would grow horizontally auxin is evenly distributed / seedling experiences gravity on all parts equally because of rotation so each side grows / elongates equally		1 1 1	AO3 4.5.4.1
11.1	0		1	AO2 4.7.2.1
11.2	8		1	AO2 4.7.2.1
11.3	all points correctly plotted **4** marks **but** at least 15 points for **3** marks **but** at least 10 points correctly plotted **2** marks **but** at least six points correctly plotted **1** mark points joined up to make a 'kite'	allow ± half a small square	4	AO2 4.7.2.1
11.4	**Level 2:** A detailed and coherent argument is given, which explains why species B and D are more common on the path and why species A and C are more common away from the path.		3–4	AO3 4.7.1.1 4.7.2.1
	Level 1: Discrete relevant points are made, although the arguments may not be clear.		1–2	
	No relevant content		0	
	Indicative content • species A and C are tall(er) • species A and C are killed by mowing on the path • species A and C can survive away from the path as they are tall enough to successfully compete for light • species B and D are low-growing • species B and D are not killed by mowing on the path / are missed by the mower • species B and D cannot survive away from the path as they are not tall enough to successfully compete for light			

Question	Answer(s)	Extra info	Mark(s)	AO/Spec ref.
12.1	**Level 3:** A coherent evaluation is given, with relevant details, which demonstrates an understanding of the principles of investigations and analysis of results.		5–6	AO3 4.5.2.1
	Level 2: An evaluation is given with mostly relevant detail, which demonstrates a reasonable understanding of the relevant principles. The evaluation may not be completely logical and may be missing some detail.		3–4	
	Level 1: Discrete relevant points are made which demonstrate some understanding of the relevant principles.		1–2	
	No relevant content		0	
	Indicative content **Method** • only recording the shortest time for each student is not as representative as taking the mean result for each student • only using the right hand means that some students may not be using their dominant hand • different numbers of girls and boys is taken into account by taking mean results • sample sizes are small **Conclusion** • it is correct that the mean time for the girls is less than for the boys • the results for the boys show more variation than for the girls • if the longest boys' result (0.32) is discounted then boys overall have the shortest reaction time • the conclusion is based on a small sample size • the conclusion should only apply to this way of measuring reaction time			
12.2	receptor = ear effector = hand muscles		1 1	AO2 4.5.2.1
12.3	electric impulses along neurones / nerve cells		1 1	AO1 4.5.2.1
12.4	no – no mark pressing the button is a conscious action **or** pressing the button is not an automatic action		1	AO2 4.5.2.1

Question	Answer(s)	Extra info	Mark(s)	AO/Spec ref.
01.1	poison		1	AO1 4.3.3.2
01.2	mimicry – tricks animals specialised leaves – curl when touched thorns – difficult to eat all three correct for **2** marks one or two correct for **1** mark		2	AO1 4.3.3.2
01.3	skin		1	AO1 4.3.1.6
01.4	antibody production		1	AO1 4.3.1.6
01.5	middle one 		1	AO1 4.2.2.3
01.6	kill bacteria inside the body specific bacteria are killed by specific antibiotics		2	AO1 4.3.1.8.
01.7	painkillers treat the symptoms of disease but do not kill pathogens / antibiotics kill bacteria		2	AO1 4.3.1.8.
02.1	virus		1	AO1 4.3.1.2
02.2	distinctive 'mosaic' pattern of discolouration on the leaves		1	AO1 4.3.1.2
02.3	affects the growth of the plant / plant is smaller / stunted		1	AO1 4.3.1.2
02.4	black spot		1	AO1 4.3.1.4
02.5	looks yellow / lacks normal green colour because magnesium ions needed to make chlorophyll		1 1	AO1 4.3.3.1
02.6	nitrate ions needed for protein synthesis (and therefore growth)		1	AO1 4.3.3.1
03.1	enzymes		1	AO1 4.2.2.1
03.2	amino acids lipids	accept fats (instead of lipids)	1 1	AO1 4.2.2.1 4.4.2.3
03.3	amylase, buffer, starch must be correct order		1	AO2 4.2.2.1
03.4	**either** of: • buffer must be added to the enzyme before the starch is added – as the reaction will start as soon as the enzyme and starch meet • if no buffer (or added afterwards) results will not be valid as the pH will be changed after the reaction has started		1	AO2 4.2.2.1

Question	Answer(s)	Extra info	Mark(s)	AO/Spec ref.
03.5	a control makes it easier to compare colours as the water in the control doesn't contain any starch / so you can be sure all the starch is gone / digested / broken down, if it is the same colour as the control		1 1	AO2 4.2.2.1
03.6	85 + 80 + 75 = 240 240/3 = 80 seconds	Must state unit (seconds) for 3rd mark	2 1	AO1 4.2.2.1
03.7	pH 7		1	AO2 4.2.2.1
03.8	mean rate increases (or time decreases) up to a maximum at pH 7 and at a higher pH it decreases (or time increases)		1 1	AO2 4.2.2.1
04.1	animal cells, line drawn from: • plasma membrane only, no cell wall • carbohydrate stored as glycogen plant cells, line drawn from: • chloroplasts • large vacuole all four correct for **3** marks three correct for **2** marks two correct for **1** mark		3	AO1 4.1.1.2
04.2	to keep the specimen flat		1	AO1 4.1.1.2
04.3	iodine solution		1	AO1 4.1.1.2
04.4	virus bacterium red blood cell leaf cell	**all** must be in correct order for mark	1	AO1 4.1.1.1 4.1.1.2
04.5	 Meristem – region of cell division Scale bar should be approximately 10 mm long and labelled 2 mm	1 mark for drawing, with distinct meristem area 1 mark for label 1 mark for sensible units / scale 1 mark for correct scale bar	2 2	AO2 4.2.3.1 4.1.1.2
05.1	accept values in range 65 000–70 000		1	AO2 4.2.2.5 4.2.2.6

Question	Answer(s)	Extra info	Mark(s)	AO/Spec ref.
05.2	active = nearly 4000 incidences (allow ± 1000) drink less alcohol = 12 000 incidences (allow ± 1000) and therefore drinking less alcohol produced about three times fewer cancers as being active	**1 mark** for both readings must include the comparison for second mark	1 1	AO3 4.2.2.5 4.2.2.6
05.3	men and women are exposed to different environmental factors	accept that men and women have structural and genetic differences	1	AO3 4.2.2.5 4.2.2.6 4.2.2.7
05.4	eat fruit and veg lots of fibre low salt low processed / red meat low alcohol	must include low alcohol for **2 marks** (to reward recognising alcohol / drinks are part of the diet) and at least two others	2	AO2 4.2.2.6 4.2.2.7
05.5	lung cancer	accept lung by itself	1	AO1 4.2.2.6
05.6	benign tumours are: any **one** of: • growths of abnormal cells • contained in one area • usually within a membrane • do not invade other parts of the body malignant tumour cells are cancers plus any **one** of: • invade neigh-bouring tissues • spread to differ-ent parts of the body • spread in the blood • form secondary tumours	must link malignant tumours to being cancers	1 2	AO1 4.2.2.7
06.1	white blood cells are producing antibodies in response to the presence of Lumpius / pathogen / vaccination	accept lymphocytes accept detect antigens on dead / inactive Lumpius	1	AO2 4.3.1.6 4.3.1.7

Question	Answer(s)	Extra info	Mark(s)	AO/Spec ref.
06.2	any **two** of: • white blood cells instantly recognise live Lumpius / pathogen (because it has the same antigens as the vaccine) • and respond **more quickly** to the infection by producing many specific antibodies • which lock onto the Lumpius / pathogen and kill them before the person becomes ill / person is immune / has immunity	accept lymphocytes must state 'more quickly' or equivalent	2	AO2 4.3.1.6 4.3.1.7
06.3	yes, **because** many specific antibodies are produced, more quickly when volunteers are infected with live Lumpius / pathogen	must state yes (no marks awarded if say no)	2	AO3 4.3.1.9
06.4	clinical trial many volunteers recruited / tested on many humans		1 1	AO3 4.3.1.9
06.5	infectious diseases allergies	accept skin rashes or asthma for second mark	1 1	AO1 4.2.2.5
07.1	oxygen		1	AO1 4.4.1.2
07.2	by counting the number of bubbles produced in 1 minute	accept other sensible period of time must mention time for second mark	2	AO2 4.4.1.2
07.3	graduated syringe	accept measuring syringe	1	AO2 4.4.1.2
07.4	any **two** of: • ruler / other measuring device • clock / watch • thermometer • gas syringe • measuring cylinder		2	AO2 4.4.1.2

Question	Answer(s)	Extra info	Mark(s)	AO/Spec ref.
07.5	**Level 3:** A detailed and coherent explanation is provided with most of the relevant content, which demonstrates a comprehensive understanding of the investigation and the order in which it is carried out. The response gives logical steps, with reasons.		5–6	**AO2** 4.4.1.2
	Level 2: A detailed and coherent explanation is provided. The student has a broad understanding of the investigation. The response makes mainly logical steps with some reasoning.		3–4	
	Level 1: Simple descriptions of the investigation are made along with reference to photosynthesis. The response demonstrates limited logical linking of points.		1–2	
	No relevant content		0	
	Indicative content • set up apparatus as in diagram • make sure plant is photosynthesising (can see bubbles of oxygen) • measure and record the temperature of water in beaker; the water is intended to maintain a constant temperature, so the temperature should be taken periodically and kept constant; controlling other variables • measure and place lamp a specified distance from apparatus – control of light intensity related to distance of lamp from apparatus • carry out at several different distances of lamp (five distances) • allow plant to acclimatise to each new distance of the lamp / light intensity (2 mins) • record production rate of oxygen – count bubbles over given time period – 1 min / 5 mins, at each distance • repeat three times for each distance of the lamp / light intensity • calculate mean production oxygen rate			
07.6	lots of sunshine = lots of oxygen produced / high rate of photosynthesis and therefore lots of oxygen = good for fish in pond	allow converse lack of sunshine / in shady area = lower rate of photosynthesis / less oxygen produced allow converse in shade = not so good for fish	1 1	**AO3** 4.4.1.2

Question	Answer(s)	Extra info	Mark(s)	AO/Spec ref.
08.1	heart rate increasing		2	**AO2** 4.4.2.2
08.2	breath volume increasing		2	**AO2** 4.4.2.2
08.3	oxygenated blood supply to muscles increasing		2	**AO2** 4.4.2.2
08.4	anaerobic		1	**AO1** 4.4.2.1
08.5	lactic acid		1	**AO1** 4.4.2.2 4.4.2.1
08.6	person B		1	**AO3** 4.4.2.2
08.7	any **two** of: for person B: • heart rate increases more slowly / doesn't increase as fast • heart rate reaches a lower steady state • decreases more quickly after exercise / recovers more quickly / returns to resting rate quicker	allow converse for person A allow reaches a lower maximum allow converse for person A allow converse for person A must be clear which person is being referred to	2	**AO3** 4.4.2.2
09.1	chloroplast		1	**AO2** 4.1.1.2
09.2	**Level 3:** A detailed and coherent description is provided with most of the relevant content, which demonstrates a comprehensive understanding of photosynthesis. The response is logical.		5–6	**AO1** 4.4.1.1 4.4.1.2 4.4.1.3
	Level 2: A detailed and coherent description is provided. The student has a broad understanding of photosynthesis. The response makes mainly logical steps with some linkage.		3–4	
	Level 1: Simple descriptions of photosynthesis are made. The response demonstrates limited logical linking of points.		1–2	
	No relevant content		0	

Question	Answer(s)	Extra info	Mark(s)	AO/Spec ref.

	Indicative content
	describe photosynthesis:
	• carbon dioxide + water light → glucose + oxygen
	• endothermic reaction
	• energy is transferred from the environment
	• to the chloroplasts by light
	the factors that affect it:
	• rate of photosynthesis affected by:
	  ○ temperature
	  ○ light intensity
	  ○ carbon dioxide concentration
	  ○ amount of chlorophyll
	and how plants use the products:
	• glucose produced converted to starch, fats and oils for storage
	• used for respiration
	• used to produce cellulose, which strengthens the cell wall
	• used to produce amino acids for protein synthesis.
		accept CO_2, H_2O, O_2 and $C_6H_{12}O_6$		

09.3	independent variable: salt concentration dependent variable: (change in) mass of potato cylinder		1 1	AO2 4.1.3.2
10.1	accept answers in order of 25 cm²	second mark for correct units	2	AO3 4.1.3.1
10.2	$(228/25) \times 100 = 912\%$ allow error carried forward from 10.1	2 marks for calculation (ecf) third mark for 3 significant figures	3	AO3 4.1.3.1
10.3	Fennec foxes have larger ears so there is a larger surface area to lose heat from	allow converse (Arctic foxes have small ears (small surface area) to conserve heat) for 1 mark	2	AO3 4.1.3.1

Set B – Paper 2

Question	Answer(s)	Extra info	Mark(s)	AO/Spec ref.
01.1	abiotic		1	AO 1 4.7.1.1
01.2	any two from: • light • space • water • mineral ions	do not accept food	2	AO 1 4.7.1.1
01.3	any two from: • food • territory • water	do not accept space	2	AO 1 4.7.1.1
01.4	interdependence		1	AO 1 4.7.1.1
01.5	a community in which all the species and environmental factors are in balance so that population sizes remain fairly constant		1 1	AO 1 4.7.1.1
01.6	methane		1	AO1 4.7.2.3
01.7	carbon dioxide mineral ions		2	AO1 4.7.2.2
02.1	nerves: • fast acting • acts for short time • acts in a specific area • electrical hormones: • slow acting • acts for long time • acts more generally • chemical	for each mark, a line must be drawn from each of the opposing descriptions; i.e. for first mark one line drawn from fast acting to nervous system and one line drawn from slow acting to hormonal system (1 mark)	4	AO1 4.5.2.1 4.5.3.1
02.2	$85 + 87 + 83 + 81 = 336$ $336/4 = 84$ ms	must state units for third mark	1 1 1	AO3 4.5.2.1
02.3	as more alcohol is consumed, reaction times increase, e.g. with 0.5 units / half a can, mean reaction time is 33 ms, increasing to 84 ms with 6 units / cans of beer	reference must be made to figures / results for second mark, as candidates asked to use the results	2	AO3 4.5.2.1
02.4	2000 people used as part of the study, increases repeatability (in 2nd study) / too few volunteers (in first study) lack of repeats in first study = less repeatable		1 1	AO3 4.5.2.1

Question	Answer(s)	Extra info	Mark(s)	AO/Spec ref.
03.1	sensible scales on correct axis		1	AO3 4.5.3.2
	correctly plotting points		1	
	drawing line – joining points or line of best fit		1	
	labels on axis – y axis – percentage of population who have Type 2 diabetes (%), and x axis – mean body mass (kg)		1	
03.2	correlation / positive correlation, as mean body mass increases so does percentage / incidence of type 2 diabetes		1	AO3 4.5.3.2
03.3	C – during exhalation – water leaves the body via the lungs		1	AO1 4.5.3.3
	A – when you sweat – water, ions and urea leave the body via the skin		1	
	B – when you urinate – water, ions and urea are removed via the kidneys		1	
03.4	kidney		1	AO1 4.5.3.3
03.5	either: **oral** contraceptives that contain hormones to **inhibit FSH production** so that **no eggs mature** or **Oral contraceptives / Injection /** implant / skin patch of slow release **progesterone / oral contraceptive of oestrogen and progesterone** to maintain the uterus lining and so prevent the menstrual cycle, therefore **inhibiting the maturation / release of eggs**	must state two of three emboldened text (or equivalent) must relate to only **one** method (i.e. not a mix of methods)	2	AO1 4.5.3.5
04.1	zebrafish		1	AO3 4.6.4
04.2	fugu and green spotted puffer		1	AO3 4.6.4

The graph in 03.1 shows: y axis "proportion of the population who have Type 2 diabetes (%)" with values 4.5, 5, 5.5, 6, 6.5, 7, 7.5; x axis "mean body mass /kg" with values 72 73 74 75 76 77 78 79 80; key "mean body mass".

Question	Answer(s)	Extra info	Mark(s)	AO/Spec ref.
04.3	167.7 million years ago	must give units accept mya	1	AO3 4.6.4
04.4	insufficient evidence currently to be more accurate		1	AO3 4.6.3.2 4.6.4
04.5	either: fossils or DNA profiling or antibiotic resistance (in case of bacteria)		1	AO1 4.6.3.4 4.6.3.5
04.6	**Level 3:** A detailed and coherent explanation is provided with most of the relevant content, which demonstrates a comprehensive understanding of speciation and how medaka and stickleback may have become separate species. The response gives logical steps, with reasons.		5-6	AO2 4.6.2.1 4.6.2.2 4.6.3.1 4.6.3.2
	Level 2: A detailed and coherent explanation is provided. The student has a broad understanding of speciation and refers to medaka and stickleback. The response makes mainly logical steps with some reasoning.		3-4	
	Level 1: Simple descriptions of speciation are made along with reference to the medaka and stickleback. The response demonstrates limited logical linking of points.		1-2	
	No relevant content		0	
	Indicative content • definition of species as organisms that are able to interbreed to produce fertile offspring • barriers separate ancestral species so they are no longer able to breed • most commonly physical / geological, can also be reproductive or ecological, examples given should be in relation to fish, e.g. river split course, courtship behaviour, changes in pH or salinity • 96-150 mya stickleback and medaka had a common ancestor that was a different species from either of them • this fish species got separated into two groups • random mutations occur in each isolated group of fish / different mutations in each group • the fish best suited to the environment survive and pass on their genes			

Question	Answer(s)	Extra info	Mark(s)	AO/Spec ref.
	• if the environment is different, for each group of fish, selection pressure means that different mutations are favoured by natural selection • over a long period of time • different characteristics will develop in the different fish groups • if the barrier were removed / the fish were able to mix again, they would no longer be able to breed and so are considered separate species			
05.1	cerebral cortex		1	**AO1** 4.5.2.2
05.2	cerebellum		1	**AO1** 4.5.2.2
05.3	medulla		1	**AO1** 4.5.2.2
05.4	A – complex functions e.g. learning, memory, emotion and conscious thought B – unconscious / automatic functions e.g. movement and balance C – unconscious / automatic (and homeostatic), e.g. swallowing, digestion and vomiting, breathing and heart rate	allow specific example of complex function **1** mark for general function plus second mark for example, for each area	2 2 2	**AO2** 4.5.2.2
05.5	as animal increases in weight so does the size of their brain	accept bigger animals have bigger brains accept reverse	1	**AO3** 4.5.1 4.5.2.1
05.6	either: • a larger animal requires a bigger brain to control / coordinate its living processes or • metabolism of animal / energy demands of brain limits brain size so if the animal is larger it is able to support the energy requirements of a larger brain		1	**AO2** 4.5.1 4.5.2.1
06.1	heterozygous		1	**AO2** 4.6.1.6
06.2	mice A and B		1	**AO2** 4.6.1.6
06.3	brown		1	**AO2** 4.6.1.6

Question	Answer(s)	Extra info	Mark(s)	AO/Spec ref.
06.4	any three of: gamete would contain brown fur allele from Mouse B and white fur allele from Mouse C offspring would receive one of each / one brown fur allele and one white fur allele a dominant allele is always expressed, even if only one copy is present brown fur gene is dominant and therefore expressed / offspring are brown furred a recessive allele is only expressed if two copies are present (therefore no dominant allele present)		3	**AO2** 4.6.1.6
06.5	**Level 3**: A detailed and coherent explanation is provided with most of the relevant content, which demonstrates a comprehensive understanding of the structure of DNA. The response gives logical steps, with reasons.		5-6	**AO1** 4.6.1.4 4.6.1.5
	Level 2: A detailed and coherent explanation is provided. The student has a broad understanding of the structure of DNA. The response makes mainly logical steps with some reasoning.		3-4	
	Level 1: Simple descriptions of the structure of DNA are made. The response demonstrates limited logical linking of points.		1-2	
	No relevant content		0	
	Indicative content • DNA is found in the cell nucleus • DNA is a polymer made up of two strands forming a double helix • the DNA is contained in structures called chromosomes • a gene is a small section of DNA on a chromosome • each gene codes for a particular sequence of amino acids, to make a specific protein • DNA is made from four different nucleotides • each nucleotide consists of a common sugar and phosphate group with one of four different bases attached to the sugar • the order of bases controls the order in which amino acids are assembled to produce a particular protein • three bases code for a particular amino acid • bases always pair C and G, A and T • the long strands of DNA consist of alternating sugar and phosphate sections			

Question	Answer(s)	Extra info	Mark(s)	AO/Spec ref.
07.1	any one from: • green plants • algae / weed • producers / primary producers		1	**AO2** 4.7.2.1 4.7.4.1
07.2	*T. sarasinorum* numbers increase and they eat lots of fish eggs		1	**AO2** 4.7.1.1 4.7.1.3 4.7.2.1
	therefore fewer fish survive from the eggs and there are fewer to eat, so 'elongated' eats more shrimp		1	
	'thicklip' numbers decrease as they are now in direct competition for shrimp, not enough shrimp for all		1	
07.3	live in different habitats (1 mark only)		1	**AO2** 4.7.1.1 4.7.2.1
	T. opudi lives in bush cover and rocks, whereas *T. wahjui* lives on the muddy bottom		1	
07.4	any one from: • sewage • fertilizer run-off • toxic chemicals		1	**AO1** 4.7.3.2
07.5	energy (/stored in biomass) is lost at each stage		1	**AO1** 4.7.4.2 4.7.4.3
	through waste products, respiration, movement and maintaining a constant body temperature		1	
	therefore there is insufficient energy to maintain another population at the top		1	
08.1	A – nucleus containing DNA removed from egg cell B – electric pulse causes skin cell to fuse with egg cell C – cell fusion D – cell division E – (early-stage) embryo is implanted into surrogate		5	**AO2** 4.6.2.5
08.2	variation		1	**AO2** 4.6.2.1
08.3	any one from: • Aphids / other named insect that reproduces asexually • Malarial parasite in human host • Fungi • Bulbs eg daffodils • Runners eg strawberries • Any other correct example		1	**AO1** 4.6.1.1
08.4	any two from: • only one parent needed • more time and energy efficient as do not need to find a mate • faster than sexual reproduction • many identical offspring can be produced when conditions are favourable • genetically identical, so if parent is well adapted to environment offspring will be too		2	**AO1** 4.6.1.3

Question	Answer(s)	Extra info	Mark(s)	AO/Spec ref.
08.5	selective breeding		1	**AO2** 4.6.2.3
08.6	genetic engineering		1	**AO2** 4.6.2.4
08.7	the gardener's method: • is the traditional method of breeding together individuals with desired characteristics • is the more natural method • takes a long time (many generations); offspring won't definitely have trait the gardener wants		1 (one point required)	**AO2** 4.6.2.3 4.6.2.4
	the farmer's method: • is more technical • is faster by transplanting specific genes for desired characteristics • is more expensive • offspring will definitely have the desired traits		1 (one point required)	
09.1	population size means the number of individuals of a species that live in a habitat (number)		1	**AO1** 4.7.1.1
	population density is the number of individuals in a given / specific area		1	
09.2	transect		1	**AO2** 4.7.1.1
09.3	systematic sampling: at regular intervals (e.g. every 50 cm)		1	**AO2** 4.7.1.1
	intervals must be sufficient to capture the changes in vegetative cover		1	
09.4	construct further transects at 10m intervals / other sensible distance down the path		1	**AO2** 4.7.1.1
	take quadrats at the same distances as before (as suggested in Q09.3) along these transects		1	
	calculate the means at each quadrant place along the length of the path (add up all the plantains and divide by number of quadrants along the length of the path) to give mean number across the path		1	
09.5	plants complete with each other for limited resources / many plants at verge, lots of competition		1	**AO3** 4.7.1 4.7.1.3 4.7.1.4
	plantain leaves are tough / have adapted to being trampled and may out-compete more delicate plants, which are trampled in the middle of the path		1	